Pupils with Learning Difficulties in Mainstream Schools

Christina Tilstone, Penny Lacey, Jill Porter and Christopher Robertson

Da   ers

David Fulton Publishers Ltd
Ormond House, 26–27 Boswell Street, London WCIN 3JZ

www.fultonpublishers.co.uk

First published in Great Britain by David Fulton Publishers 2000
Reprinted 2000

Note: The rights of Christina Tilstone, Penny Lacey, Jill Porter and Christopher Robertson to
be identified as the authors of this work have been asserted by them in accordance with the
Copyright, Designs and Patents Act 1988.

Copyright © David Fulton Publishers Ltd 2000

British Library Cataloguing in Publication Data
A catalogue record for this book is available from the British Library.

ISBN 1-8534–586–0

Typeset by Textype Typesetters, Cambridge
Printed in Great Britain by The Cromwell Press Ltd, Trowbridge, Wilts.

Contents

Acknowledgements

We would like to thank the pupils, the staff of the schools and the parents with whom we have worked. They have taught us so much and been a constant source of inspiration.

We also wish to thank Pat Dolan for sharing insights into her daughter's education, and BILD (British Institute of Learning Disabilities) for permission to reproduce some aspects of Mabel's life from Atkinson, Jackson and Walmsley (1997) *Forgotten Lives: Exploring the History of Learning Disability.*

Foreword

Each publication in this series of books is concerned with approaches to intervention with children with specific needs in mainstream schools. In this preface we provide a backdrop of general issues concerning special needs in mainstream schools. The government's recent Action Programme, published after considering responses to the Special Educational Needs (SEN) Green Paper, will lead to changes in practice in the future. Following consultation, there will be a revised and simplified Code of Practice in place by the school year 2000/2001. It is intended that this will make life easier.

The SEN Code of Practice (DfE 1994a), following the 1993 Education Act, provides practical guidance to LEAs and school governing bodies on their responsibilities towards pupils with SEN. Schools and LEAs were required to regard its recommendations from September 1994. The Department for Education also issued Circular 6/94 (DfE 1994b) which provided suggestions as to how schools should manage their special needs provision alongside that made by other local schools. These documents embody the twin strategies of individual pupil support and whole-school development. The Green Paper *Excellence for All* also seeks to promote the development of more sophisticated and comprehensive forms of regional and local planning (DfEE 1997).

The Code of Practice, with its staged approach to assessment supervised within each mainstream school by a teacher designated as Special Educational Needs Coordinator (SENCO), was widely welcomed.

For example, Walters (1994) argued that 'this Code of Practice builds on good practice developed over the ten years and heralds a "new deal" for children with special needs in the schools of England and Wales'. But he also reflected worries that, in the light of other developments, the process might provide an added incentive for schools to dump their 'problem children into the lap of the LEA' rather than devising strategies to improve behaviour in the school environment. Such children, he feared, were in danger of being increasingly marginalised.

Impact on teachers

While receiving a mainly positive welcome for its intentions, the *Code of Practice* (DfE 1994a) also raised some concerns about its impact on teachers who became responsible for its implementation. On the positive side the Code would raise the profile of special needs and establish a continuum of provision in mainstream schools. There was a clear specification of different types of special educational need and the Code's emphasis was on meeting them through individual programmes developed in cooperation with parents.

However, there were possible problems in meeting the challenge of establishing effective and time-efficient procedures for assessment and monitoring. Further challenges were to be found in making best use of resources and overcoming barriers to liaison with parents.

Anxieties about the Code

Following the introduction of the Code these anxieties were confirmed by a number of research studies of teachers' perceptions of the impact of the Code. The picture which emerged from these studies showed appreciation of the potential benefits of implementing the Code but widespread anxiety, based on early experience, about the practicalities of making it work.

Loxley and Bines (1995) interviewed head teachers and SENCOs about their views on emergent issues related to the complexities of introducing Individual Education Plans (IEPs), particularly in secondary schools.

Teachers feared that 'excessive proceduralism' could lead to the distribution of resources being skewed towards meeting the needs of children whose parents are best able to understand and exercise their rights, at the expense of provision for children whose parents are less assertive and confident. Teachers were most concerned about the allocation of scarce resources and the increased responsibilities of SENCOs for managing a system likely to reduce time for direct teaching of children.

School perspectives

Most schools were optimistic about their ability to implement the Code and positive about LEA guidelines and training, but there was less certainty that the Code would improve the education of pupils with SEN.

Asked to give their opinion on advantages and disadvantages of the Code, teachers cited as positive effects:

- a more structured framework,
- growing awareness of accountability,
- a higher profile for SEN issues,
- earlier identification,
- greater uniformity in practice, and
- increased parental involvement.

The disadvantages cited were:

- lack of resources and time,
- substantially increased workloads for all teachers as well as SENCOs,
- more time used for liaison and less for teaching.

(Rhodes 1996)

Four themes

A national survey commissioned by the National Union of Teachers (NUT) identified four themes:

1. broad support for the principles and establishment of the Code of Practice;
2. concern about the feasibility of its implementation, given a lack of time and resources;
3. problems in some areas related to perceived inadequacy of LEA support;
4. inadequate status and lack of recognition for the SENCO role.

(Lewis et al. 1996)

Another study found patchy support for SENCOs. There were wide variations in the amount of time dedicated to the role, the amount of support from head teachers and governors, involvement in decision-making, the extent of training and the degree of bureaucracy within LEAs.

SEN Register and Staged Assessment Procedures

Although its widespread adoption makes it appear to have been a national prescription, the five-stage model suggested in the Code is not a legal requirement. The Code actually states that: 'to give specific help to children who have special educational needs, schools should adopt a staged response'. (DfE 1994a, 2.20)

It goes on to indicate that some schools and LEAs may adopt different models but that, while it was not essential that there should be five stages, it was essential that there should be differentiation between the stages, aimed at matching action taken to the pupil's needs at each stage.

Five Key Stages

Nonetheless, the normal expectation is that assessment and intervention will be organised and recorded in an SEN Register for which the SENCO is responsible. The following description briefly summarises usual practice, with Stages 1–3 school-based and Stages 4 and 5 the responsibility of the LEA.

Stage 1
Class teacher identifies pupils with learning difficulty and, with support from the SENCO, attempts to meet the pupil's SEN.

Stage 2
Class teacher reports continued concern and SENCO takes responsibility for the special response to meet the pupil's SEN.

Stage 3
SENCO organises support from external agencies to help in meeting the pupil's SEN.

Stage 4
The LEA is approached by the school with a request for statutory assessment.

Stage 5
The LEA considers the need for a Statement of SEN and completes the assessment procedure; monitoring and review of the statement is organised by the LEA.

Each book in this series, explains how this process works in relation to different disabilities and difficulties as they were described in the 1981 Act and shows how individual needs can be identified and met through IEPs. While forthcoming revision of the Code may alter the details of the stages, the principles of the practices through which needs are specified will remain the same.

Information for colleagues, governors and parents

Ensuring that the school provides all necessary information for staff, governors and parents is another major element of the SENCO role. *The Organisation of Special Educational Provision* (Circular 6/94) (DfE 1994b) sets out the issues which the school should address about its SEN provision, policies and partnerships with bodies beyond the school.

This is information that must be made available and may be found in school brochures or prospectuses, in annual reports to parents and in policy documents. The ultimate responsibility for following the guidance in the Circular rests with the head teacher and governing body but the SENCO will be engaged with all these issues and the Circular forms in effect a useful checklist for monitoring the development and implementation of the SEN policy.

You may find it useful to consider the following points as a way of familiarising yourself with provision in your school.

Basic information about the school's special educational provision

- Who is responsible for coordinating the day-to-day provision of education for pupils with SEN at your school (whether or not the person is known as the SEN Coordinator)?

- Arrangements need to be made for coordinating the provision of education for pupils with SEN. Does your school's SENCO work alone or is there a coordinating or support team?
- What are the admission arrangements for pupils with SEN who do not have a statement and is there any priority for SEN admissions?
- What kind of provision does your school have for the special educational needs in which it specialises?
- What are your school's access arrangements for pupils with physical and sensory disabilities?

Information about the school's policies for the identification, assessment and provision for all pupils with SEN

- What is your school policy on allocation of money for SEN resources?
- How are pupils with SEN identified and their needs determined and reviewed? How are parents told about this?
- What does your school policy say about arrangements for providing access for pupils with SEN to a balanced and broadly-based curriculum (including the National Curriculum)?
- What does your school policy say about 'integration arrangements'? How do pupils with SEN engage in the activities of the school together with pupils who do not have special educational needs.
- How does your school demonstrate the effective implementation of its SEN policy? How does the governing body evaluate the success of the education which is provided at the school for pupils with SEN?
- What are the arrangements made by the governing body relating to the treatment of complaints from parents of pupils with SEN concerning the provision made at the school?
- What are your school's 'time targets' for response to complaints?

Information about the school's staffing policies and partnership with bodies beyond the school

- What is your school's policy on continuing in-service professional training for staff in relation to special educational needs?
- What are your school's arrangements regarding the use of teachers and facilities from outside the school, including links with support services for special educational needs?
- What is the role played by the parents of pupils with SEN? Is there a 'close working, relationship'?
- Do you have any links with other schools, including special schools, and is there provision made for the transition of pupils with SEN between schools or between the school and the next stage of life or education?

• How well does 'liaison and information exchange' work in your school, e.g. links with health services, social services and educational welfare services and any voluntary organisations which work on behalf of children with SEN?

In any school those arrangements which are generally available to meet children's learning needs will have an impact on those services which are required to meet specific needs. It is therefore very important that a reader of any one of this series of specialist books makes reference to the general situation in their school when thinking about ways of improving the learning situation for pupils.

Harry Daniels and Colin Smith
University of Birmingham
February 1999

References

Crowther, D., Dyson, A. *et al.* (1997) *Implemention of the Code of Practice: The Role of the Special Educational Needs Coordinator.* Special Needs Research Centre, Department of Education, University of Newcastle upon Tyne.

Department for Education (DfE) (1994a) *Code of Practice on the Identification and Assessment of Special Educational Needs.* London:HMSO.

Department for Education (DfE) (1994b) *The Organisation of Special Educational Provision.* Circular 6/94. London: HMSO.

Department for Education and Employment (DfEE) (1997) *Excellence for All: Meeting Special Educational Needs.* London: HMSO.

Hornby, G. (1995) 'The Code of Practice: boon or burden', *British Journal of Special Education* 22(3) 116–119

Lewis, A., Neill, S. R. St J. and Campbell, R. J. (1996) *The Implementation of the Code of Practice in Primary and Secondary School: A National Survey of the Perceptions of Special Educational Needs Coordinators.* The University of Warwick.

Loxley, A. and Bines, H. (1995) 'Implementing the Code of Practice: professional responses', *Support for Learning* 10(4) 185–189.

Rhodes, L. W. (1996) 'Code of Practice: first impressions', *Special!* Spring 1996.

Walters, B. (1994) *Management of Special Needs.* London: Cassell.

Part I Rationale and Framework for Teaching and Learning

This book is concerned with promoting positive practice in mainstream schools for pupils with a wide range of learning difficulties. Immediately we face a dilemma as the targeting of a particular group of learners in this way suggests that we are proposing that they should be considered different from other pupils, requiring specialist support and teaching techniques. Our approach to learning difficulties is not that they should be viewed as a collection of deficits which are intrinsic to an individual or group, but as additional learning needs that exist in particular contexts. Many learning difficulties can actually be created by an education system that has grown up over the years and failed to be responsive to diversity. We hope that the content of this book will enable teachers to recognise shared as well as exceptional needs and to develop their professional skills in a way that promotes effective learning for **all** pupils.

Part I provides a rationale and framework for teaching pupils with learning difficulties in mainstream schools. It illustrates how the acceptance of people with learning difficulties into society depends on the flexibility of teachers and other professionals in mainstream settings and their ability to respond to diversity and to reject labels and stereotypical images.

The content of Chapter 1 emphasises the need for high expectations and a positive attitude in providing teaching and learning experiences of pupils with learning difficulties. A key element of this lies with the importance of focusing on the strengths of pupils rather than their difficulties. In Chapter 2 the emphasis is broadened to a consideration of adaptations to the curriculum to meet needs through structured approaches. The importance of working collaboratively is highlighted and discussed in detail in Part II.

As the above indicates, the ethos of teaching pupils with learning difficulties is examined in Part I, but there are additional characteristics which are emphasised throughout. The importance of ensuring that pupils (who in the past may have been disenfranchised by the education system) feel valued and respected as learners is an important theme running throughout Part I. Pupils need to be involved in all decisions to meet their special educational needs, and if staff are willing and able to listen to their opinions it is more likely that an appropriate curriculum will be developed. Finally, the fundamental requirement for teachers to extend their knowledge and existing skills through a reflective and analytical stance underpins the ethos of teaching pupils with learning difficulties.

CHAPTER 1

Introduction

Setting the scene

For people like me and a lot more you know, people were frightened of us. So in them days they said OK, there's nowhere for you, you get shut away in big institutions. If people are different then other people get frightened. I still see it. People are frightened of people like me, and a lot more, because we are different.

(Atkinson, Jackson and Walmsley 1987: 11)

The quotation is from the autobiography of a person with learning difficulties who lived for most of her life in a long stay hospital. Her 'schooling' took place on the wards where she participated in some craft work. In her words:

In them days they said you wasn't able enough to learn so you didn't go to school you went to like a big ward and they had tables. You just went there and made baskets or what-have you. Because in them days they said you wasn't capable enough to learn to do anything else, so that's what you did. (ibid., pp. 23–4)

Mabel was born in 1945 and, under the Regulations which followed the 1944 Education Act, she was labelled as 'educationally subnormal'. If she had been born a year or two earlier she would have been considered to be a 'mental defective' and categorised as an 'idiot' or an 'imbecile', which were the accepted terms for those whose 'mental defectiveness' was of such a degree that they were unable to guard themselves against common dangers. At the age of seven, she was sent to a residential institution were she received a 'dependent' model of care. She now lives in the community and is an active member of the self-advocacy movement. Not only is she taking her rightful place in the community, but she is making a contribution to society by speaking at conferences, running workshops and representing 'People First' (a powerful self-advocacy group for people with learning disabilities) on national and international bodies. Her experiences reflect the changes in policies and practices over the last fifty years for those who have difficulties in learning.

When Mabel was of school age she, and many others like her who were considered to be 'mentally defective', were excluded from the education system and their 'schooling', or lack of it, took place in a residential institution. She cannot remember her parents, but if her circumstances had been different, she could have lived with her family at home and attended a junior training centre. If the centre or, in Mabel's case, the long-stay hospital had been progressive, she would have done more than merely taking part in craft activities, and consequently benefited from an individualised skills-training programme in the areas of self-help, socialisation, occupation and communication.

Whatever the quality of the experiences offered to them, children placed in residential institutions or attending junior training centres were the responsibility of the Health Service until 1971 when, under the Education (Handicapped Children) Act (1970), the onus for their 'education' was transferred to the education authorities. Stevens (1997) makes the point that for mentally defective children placed in long-stay hospitals 'doctors ran institutions, nurses controlled patients, and patients were "passive" victims of the staff' (p. 52). Despite some good practice, children were likely to be 'cared for' in both the long-stay hospitals or training centres in ways which minimised meaningful experiences and resulted in reduced expectations.

Labels and categories: help or hindrance?

If Mabel had been born some twenty years later she would have had the same basic right as *all* children to 'education', although almost certainly it would have taken place in a separate special school. Mabel left the hospital in 1976 to live in a hostel; her first step into the community. Two years later the famous Warnock Committee (DES 1978) reported and alternatives to the segregated special school provision were recommended. Members of the Committee proposed that a greater number of children could be educated in mainstream schools and suggested the well-known three types of integrated provision:

- *locational*: where children attended separate special units but on the same site as mainstream school;
- *social*: where children went to separate classes but mixed with ordinary children at mealtimes, playtimes and assemblies;
- *functional*: where children attended the same classes as the non-handicapped and shared the same curriculum.

The Committee recognised that special schools played a vital role in encouraging integration, and the 1981 Education Act (DES 1981) which followed the report took the recommendations further and for the first time, it became the legal duty of every LEA to educate *all* children in ordinary schools, but only if compatible with:

- parents' wishes;
- the efficient education of other children;
- the efficient use of resources.

Only children with the most severe difficulties would, the Committee felt, need special schooling (calculated at about two per cent). Whether Mabel's difficulties were in fact 'severe' cannot now be assessed; certainly, as is often the case, they are not embedded 'within' the child, but are shaped by the policies, curriculum organisation and practices of the institution; in her case, a residential hospital. The learning context can have considerable impact and, over the last ten years, it has been recognised that **school-based** factors can be a major cause of difficulties – a point which will be explored in more detail later in this book.

The notion that a pupil's special educational needs are exacerbated by the educational experiences offered is vitally important, although it should not detract from a recognition that his or her difficulties can also stem from organic difficulties (birth damage, resulting in brain damage, for example, or a genetic disorder). In many cases it is not difficult to identify the relevant aetiological factors, but the information is only useful to the teacher if it helps to identify the educational needs of the child. Down's Syndrome, for example, one of the most common genetic cause of impaired intellectual functioning, but the physical signs and disabilities are many and varied and there is no clear relationship between them and mental abilities. Those possessing many of the medical characteristics (large tongue, short neck, slanting eyes, for example) are just as likely as those with few such characteristics to have higher levels of ability. The same could be said of Fragile X syndrome which, although the most common inherited cause of learning disability, does not invariably lead to a learning difficulty nor does it have a fixed set of physical features.

Anya Souza (1997), who attended mainstream schools, lives in the community and is in paid employment, writes of the negative effects of being labelled:

> my mother was told by the doctors that I had Down's Syndrome and would be mentally and physically handicapped for the rest of my life. It was a very negative way to describe me and what to expect from me . . . the doctor has separated me out, put a label on me . . . made everything to do with me a negative image (p. 4).

Many people with Down's Syndrome live 'ordinary' lives in the community with or without a partner. They hold down jobs, drive cars and take part in a range of leisure activities. Others may have a delay in some or all of the main areas of general development and have marked sensory and physical impairments. They, and other children, particularly those with neurological damage, may be considered to have severe learning difficulties which can be identified by marked limitations in learning across all aspects of development, particularly in the area of communication, and it is this information that is important to the teacher and other members of the school staff.

The numbers of children with learning difficulties being educated full- and part-time in mainstream provision has markedly increased over the years, although the numbers vary from one LEA to another and teachers in mainstream schools are likely to encounter more and more children with a wide range of learning difficulties. As pupils with Down's Syndrome are an easily identifiable group; their placement in mainstream schools often indicates an LEA's commitment to the principle of inclusion (see Lorenz 1998a for a useful guide to the inclusion of pupils with Down's Syndrome in mainstream schools). Small-scale studies on these pupils show an increased trend towards mainstream attendance although there is a gradual decline in the numbers of pupils with Down's Syndrome in secondary schools (Lorenz 1995; O'Hanlon and Turner 1998).

Not only has the number of children with learning difficulties increased in mainstream schools, but the ways in which they are included has also developed beyond the three types of integration first described by the Warnock Committee. In addition to full-time placement in a mainstream school and attendance within a unit for children with either specified or general special needs, the range of opportunities for education to take place in mainstream settings has expanded significantly. The arrangements now include integrated nursery provision; the placement of classes of children from a special school within a mainstream school; extended and flexible links between mainstream and special schools; and many variations of these structures.

Adrian benefits from one such arrangement. In his case, the special school, where he is registered, is part of a mainstream secondary school. In real terms this means that there are two classes of pupils with learning difficulties within the mainstream school who are managed and run by the special school staff. The special school has maintained its identity within the mainstream school and pupils attend lessons in both schools. Adrian has Down's Syndrome and it is encouraging (in view of the small-scale studies mentioned above) that his secondary education is taking place in a mainstream setting. His learning difficulties have been described as moderate to severe.

Adrian

Adrian is thirteen years old and is good at languages. He attends a number of lessons in the mainstream school, particularly in German and French. In addition, he goes to mainstream assemblies and 'tutor group' sessions. He is good at reading, although his understanding is greater than his decoding ability. He is a sociable young man with friends in his own special school class and in the mainstream tutor group. He would like to join his mainstream peers in games of football at lunch-time, but when he found he could not keep up with the pace of the game he organised his own matches with friends from his special school class, which take place alongside the faster games played by his mainstream friends.

His language lessons are differentiated and he is offered extra support. In his German lesson, for example, Adrian sits next to his learning support assistant and, with her encouragement, joins in the 'quick-fire' vocabulary session at the beginning of each lesson. He answers questions in German, repeats words and phrases, puts up his hand in order to respond to the general questions asked of the group and is an accepted part of the class. The teacher differentiates in her expectations by accepting one-word answers from Adrian and phrases from the rest of the class. The learning support assistant occasionally helps him with a word or repeats the question directly to him in order that he hears it correctly.

Adrian's teachers and parents are pleased with his progress and feel that he has gained from peer-group involvement in several ways. His self-esteem has risen, for example, and his social skills have improved. He can now cope with greater pressure, and it is very likely that the time he spends in mainstream classes could increase.

What can be learned from this brief description? First, major reasons for Adrian's progress are the flexible arrangements which have been created to allow him to 'dip into' appropriate lessons within the mainstream school. Good communication between the two sets of staff has enabled the provision of the best possible curriculum 'mix' in order to meet his needs. These will change over time, and as his skills develop it is likely that more of his education will be provided in the mainstream.

The second reason for his progress can be attributed to the emphasis on enhancing his achievements. German and French are his 'strengths' which have been recognised and celebrated. Such a positive response has almost certainly contributed to his rise in self-esteem and to the recognition that he is respected and valued. Although specialised teaching takes place in both settings, his lessons in the special class enable him to acquire the basic skills in the subject areas which are not considered to be his present strengths and at a pace which is suited to his learning style (see Chapter 4 for a more detailed discussion).

The learning support assistant's skills enable Adrian to access the lessons and to increase in self-confidence. She is aware of his slight hearing loss and acts appropriately to enable him to understand. It is estimated that the majority of children with Down's Syndrome have a hearing impairment (Fortnum *et al.* 1996), which is one of the few important messages that the 'diagnosis' brings.

The teacher not only differentiates her approach and the materials she uses, but also her expectations. Questions and tasks for Adrian are no less demanding than those for his peers, but her **differential thinking** (Hart 1996) results in high but realistic expectations and enables her to design teaching structures which are child-centred and manageable within the mainstream classroom. Finally, the way in which his learning needs are expressed are analytical and positive. There is an emphasis on 'what he can do' and 'what he needs to do next', rather than on 'what he cannot do' and is likely to have 'failed at'.

Adrian's learning difficulties are described as severe to moderate – and could perhaps have been described as mild to moderate – but what do these terms mean? Historically, in this country and in the USA, IQ scores have been used to categorise children. Table 1.1 shows the bands which corresponded to the different categories.

Table 1.1: IQ ranges for bands of learning difficulties (USA and UK)

Category	IQ range USA	IQ range UK
Mild	50–55 to approx. 70	70–75 to approx. 80
Moderate	35–40 to 50–55	50 to 70–75
Severe	20–25 to 35–40	Below 50
Profound	Below 20 or 25	

Thankfully, the use of IQ scores to classify learning needs no longer applies, and the reasons for their rejection have been succinctly summed up by Farrell (1997) as follows:

- many pupils with learning difficulties do not respond well to individual test situations and it is almost inevitable that the scores will not be reliable;
- the test may be impossible to administer as some children may have difficulties with concentration or (as in the case of Marie below) do not use a 'traditional' communication system;
- once determined, test scores are considered to be 'tablets of stone' and decisions based on them do not recognise that they can alter and change dramatically.

Nevertheless, the lack of IQ scores, misleading as they could be, has led to even more confusion as there are still no agreed definitions of learning difficulties, including criteria by which pupils can be identified as having difficulties in learning. The *Code of Practice* (DfE 1994) characterises pupils with learning difficulties as follows:

> Their general lack of academic attainment will be significantly below that of their peers. In most cases, they will have difficulties acquiring basic literacy and numeracy skills and many will have significant speech and language difficulties. Some may also have poor social skills and show signs of emotional and behavioural difficulties (p. 3).

This is hardly a useful definition for identifying learning needs, and 'general level of academic attainment significantly below that of their peers' creates the impression of there being a considerable 'difference', a factor which singled Mabel out from her fellows so many years ago, and isolated her from society. Terms like 'mild', 'moderate' and 'severe' learning difficulties are in widespread use and are understood at a general level, but Crowther, Dyson and Millward (1998) found that, in the case of moderate learning difficulties in particular, such labelling was dependent upon three factors: local definitions used within individual local education authorities; the content of the statements (particularly worrying as not all pupils considered to have 'moderate learning difficulties' are statemented); and the use of SATs (standard attainment tasks) and standardised test scores, which bring with them similar problems to those previously associated with the use of IQ tests.

In our next case study we describe provision for Marie, who has been educated full-time in mainstream schools for most of her life. She could be described as having a level of attainment **significantly** below her peers and, in some areas of her development, she is still at a very early stage. At the time of writing the number of children like Marie who are being educated **full-time** in mainstream schools is small, but with the greater emphasis on inclusion, and as the flexible arrangements and options for pupils with learning difficulties in mainstream increases, the need for appropriate teaching to take place in specialist settings will decline.

Marie can be categorised as having profound and multiple learning difficulties (PMLD) which, according to Hogg and Lambe (1988), means that she is functioning at less than one-fifth of her chronological age and has additional physical difficulties, although their definition also takes into account other limitations of vision and hearing which do not apply in Marie's case. She has been diagnosed as having Rett Syndrome (currently thought to be a fault in a gene in the X chromosome) and you will see from the following profile written by her mother that, as in Adrian's case, there is an emphasis on the things Marie can do, but her diagnosis does carry some important messages for her teachers.

Marie

Marie is now nineteen years of age and was diagnosed as having Rett Syndrome when she was two. Apart from a brief spell at a special school, she has always been educated in mainstream schools and is, at present, attending a sixth form college close to her home. Marie has a complex and challenging disability resulting in a lack of mobility and verbal communication and in learning and physical disabilities; she will be totally dependent on others for all aspects of her care for the rest of her life. Her three specific barriers to learning are a delayed response; apraxia; and hand dysfunction (a direct result of the chromosome abnormality causing stereotypical movements, often hand-wringing), which increase if she is under stress.

Despite all these difficulties, Marie's communication cuts through many barriers. She communicates choices, wishes, likes and dislikes in non-traditional ways, including actions rather than language. To communicate with her, people have to be able to use non-verbal language tailored to her needs, something her friends and support workers do very well. Over the years, she has built up close relationships and her friends will often sit for hours talking to her, and watching and waiting for her responses. A pupil at the sixth form college sums up Marie's skills:

Although she is unable to voice her opinions **in words**, her eyes express much about her thoughts.

Marie makes it quite clear when she is getting bored with a lecture: she verbalises by moaning and shows a lack of interest by closing her eyes. Although she occasionally needs a rest to help her to regain concentration, eye closing does not necessarily mean that she is tired and, if removed from the situation, she becomes cheerful again!

She, like all of us, needs her friends around her and, with over a thousand students in the college, there are plenty of opportunities for her to socialise. She gets bored easily, and frustrated when she does not have people around her or is not involved in the hectic life of being a student in the college. Her mother ends Marie's profile with the following vital comment for her teachers:

> The important thing for us as a family is to focus on her communication, on what she **can do**, not on what she cannot, or does not, do. It is important to foster and develop **her** strategies of communication and not to fit them, at this stage in her life, into the more acceptable ways in which we communicate. Our aim is for her to use her abilities better, but this aim must be defined to suit **her** needs not **ours**.

As in Adrian's case Marie's achievements are expressed in positive terms and consequently help to shape positive attitudes both among the staff and her peers. The changes in attitude that have taken place in the schools in which she has been educated have given Marie the best possible opportunity to become part of the social organisation of society. She is a valued member of her present school, she is listened to and consulted, and is able to influence the decisions made on **what** she learns and **how** she is taught.

At the age of nineteen she no longer follows the National Curriculum, but when she did her legal entitlement meant that she was actively and meaningfully participating in all subjects. A clear distinction can be made between progression **within** a subject and experiencing a subject to enhance early skill levels; a point discussed in more detail in a later chapter of this book. The following extract from *Planning the Curriculum for Pupils with Profound and Multiple Learning Difficulties* (SCAA 1996) provides a useful illustration of a specific subject enhancing basic skill acquisition:

> During a mathematics lesson, a group of Years 1, 2 and 3 pupils joined together to estimate and then measure how far cars would travel when rolled down a ramp. All the pupils worked at floor level. The careful positioning of three pupils with profound and multiple learning difficulties using wedges meant that they were very much part of the action, rolling their cars down the ramp. These pupils were responsible for releasing the cars at the top of the ramp. For them, the priorities were physical skills (release of the cars) and visual skills (tracking a moving object) in the context of a lesson where the focus was on mathematics. All participated and every pupil's contribution was valued (p. 10).

Marie is a wheelchair user with the inevitable implications for the physical environment. Her lack of mobility and her additional learning difficulties are such that she will always be totally dependent on others for all aspects of her care. Her curriculum includes therapy and feeding programmes and her full-time learning support assistants (two assistants job-share a full-time post) help to maintain the basic care needed whilst she is at school. They also provide differentiated support to her subject teachers in each lesson.

Marie benefits from an interactive environment, which Ware (1996) calls a **responsive environment**, and involves all those close to her observing her non-verbal communications and responding to them. Her methods of communication (including movements and vocalisations) although idiosyncratic can, given adequate time for observation, be accurately interpreted. She is constantly given opportunities to take the lead in interactions, to indicate choices and preferences and to respond non-verbally to those communicating with her.

Her mother quite rightly, emphasises that the focus on communication must continue. Marie, like all of us will take on new learning throughout her life and her methods of communication should continue to be moulded and shaped in order that her responses are more easily recognisable to a wide range of people. Such an approach does not devalue her own communicative strategies but ensures that she has the chance to develop diverse relationships. Her learning support assistants, her teachers and her peers need to recognise that her hand-wringing is part of the disorder, but that an understanding of its patterns and its rates can provide clues to her moods and feelings. Her mother reported that, if Marie is 'stressed', her hand movements increase in frequency. Limited hand-function, a direct consequence of the chromosome abnormality, has been improved through 'Hand use' programmes. (See Lewis and Wilson 1998 for accessible advice on particular strategies to overcome or alleviate specific difficulties.)

Marie is fortunate as her mainstream placement provides access to a wide range of social contacts. Her world is not just limited to family, a few friends and a small number of staff. She has wide contacts and many friends from whom she has gained much, but she has also been able to teach them a great deal. Their contact with her has done much to alleviate their fear and prejudice and has broken down their barriers to an acceptance of her. The children who have interacted with her in her mainstream nursery, primary, secondary and further education establishments are likely to be more accepting of those with learning difficulties in future. They have become, as Allen (1999), points out, 'the gate keepers to inclusion'.

Conclusion

We hope that the accounts of Adrian, Marie and, to some extent, Mabel, have shown that their needs are at one level unique and need to be dealt with as such; at another they are shared with some or all the pupils taught by every teacher in mainstream settings. Adrian and Marie like all children have a right to be educated in the least restrictive setting but just **being** in a mainstream school does not ensure inclusion. Their profiles illustrate that they are included as part of the culture and the curricula of the schools and that the positive and flexible attitudes of the staff and pupils have helped to decrease what Booth (1996) calls 'exclusionary pressures'. These profiles provide a starting point for a consideration of the teaching and learning of pupils with learning difficulties explored in other chapters of this book, and emphasise the sociological dimension that

> inclusive education is about responding to diversity; it is about listening to unfamiliar voices, being open, empowering all members and about celebrating 'difference' in dignified ways. (Barton 1997: 233)

It is fitting, therefore to end this introduction by considering Anya Souza's experience of mainstream schooling. The following quotation sums up her feelings about her secondary education. It is particularly pertinent in the present climate as it is at the transition from mainstream primary to secondary school when many pupils with learning difficulties are transferred to special schools. She was transferred to a special school when she was about to enter the sixth form, and already had achieved three CSEs!

> Comprehensive school was great fun. I had nice teachers, nice friends and real fun . . . I can't remember anybody at this school really picking on me. I had my friends and we did the things we wanted to together. Everyone has their friends and also the people they don't want to be in contact with and stay away from. It is no different for me than anyone else. I would say that I am a demonstration that integration into schools really works. I've been through it. . .' (Souza 1997: 7)

CHAPTER 2

The responsive curriculum

Introduction

In this chapter the educational needs of pupils with learning difficulties are considered in relation to curriculum provision in mainstream school settings. We have already noted in Chapter 1 the moves from segregated to integrated education, and more recently, moves towards the development of inclusive schools. The process of inclusive education contains many interconnected strands, but at its heart lies the curriculum which serves as the focal point for the kind of quality teaching and learning discussed in Part II of this book.

A responsive curriculum

For the curriculum to be genuinely inclusive, it needs to take serious account of educational diversity and recognise the heterogeneity of educational needs that all pupils, including those with a range of learning difficulties, present to their teachers (Wedell 1995a). If the curriculum is going to fully embrace difference then it

> should be adapted to children's needs, not vice versa. Schools should therefore provide curricular opportunities to suit children with different abilities and interests. (UNESCO 1994: 22, para. 28)

However, this should not imply that we ought to make available discrete and separate special provision for pupils experiencing difficulties in learning. This would clearly be a retrograde step, in the light of a **National** Curriculum being legislated for since 1988; an entitlement curriculum, supported by policy statements indicating that all pupils could expect to benefit from following the prescribed content. It would also be conceptually incoherent, as well as being both impractical and impossible to resource. Imagine providing something entirely different for every pupil with a special ability or difficulty? The Salamanca Statement, developed at a UNESCO world conference on special education, again points to a way forward.

> Children with special needs should receive additional instructional support in the context of **the regular curriculum, not a different curriculum**. The guiding principle should be to provide all children with the same education, providing additional support to children requiring it. (p. 22, para 29, emphasis added)

Making such curriculum provision for pupils with learning difficulties is a complex task, one that can only be effectively achieved through thoughtful and systematic professional collaboration. It requires that the concepts of curriculum **breadth**, **balance** and **relevance** are carefully considered in relation to individual pupils. It also requires that progress in learning is planned and measured in ways that truly reflect the development of the individual learner. As Norwich (1990) has noted,

> the search for a common curriculum for all which is sufficiently general and flexible to incorporate programmes with specialised additional goals for some is a continuing challenge for educators (p. 87).

The National Curriculum introduced in 1988 has long been regarded as over-detailed, rigid in design and too closely wedded to the assessment of learning outcomes that have not enabled pupils with significant learning difficulties to show evidence of their educational progress. At the same time many teachers, working in both mainstream and special schools, have worked creatively, within significant constraints, to make this unyielding curriculum work for their pupils. As part of the 1999 review of the National Curriculum, the Qualifications and Curriculum Authority (QCA) on behalf of the Department for Education and Employment (DfEE) has made new proposals (QCA 1999) which aim to ensure that by the end of the year 2000 a more inclusive curriculum will be in place. The rationale for curriculum changes presented in these proposals is promising, with emphasis being placed (pp. 2–16) on flexibility and less prescription. Particular points are worth highlighting, for they should signal a positive way forward with regard to developing curriculum provision for pupils with learning difficulties, and build on current good practice described by Carpenter, Ashdown and Bovair (1996).

QCA state that they :

- are moving from simply providing a statement on access to the National Curriculum, to **more supportive guidance on the inclusion of all pupils**;
- will produce **National Curriculum** guidelines for pupils whose **attainment** up to the age of 16 is expected to remain within the range from **below Level 1 to Level 2**;
- will produce guidance to indicate **the range and types of provision, outside the National Curriculum**, such as therapy and mobility training, which could be included in the school curriculum to meet the particular requirements of individuals or groups of pupils.

These helpful 'signals' have to be seriously acted upon, if pupils with a wide range of learning difficulties are to be included fully in mainstream schooling. It will be especially important for the needs of pupils with profound and multiple learning difficulties to be addressed and for the concept of **experience** of learning, particularly within subjects, to be clarified (Brown 1996; Grove and Peacey 1999). Curriculum content cannot simply be seen as something that is transmitted from teacher to pupil. Instead, engagement with curriculum content should be seen in terms of the extent to which a pupil is:

experiencing a learning activity;
aware of at least some of the purposes of an activity;
participating actively in an activity;
involved in the activity.

(adapted from Brown 1996: 52)

An understanding of these different types of engagement, and how they overlap, enables teaching of curriculum content to be matched carefully to the learning needs of individuals. The following example illustrates this.

School visit to a cathedral – linked to the teaching of Religious Education, Geography and History

Manjula, is a seven-year-old pupil with profound and multiple learning difficulties. It is hard for her teacher and caregivers to know when Manjula is learning because she does not use speech or any kind of sign language. However, by including her in the visit to the cathedral they are providing her with important experiences, shared with other children. In fact, these experiences give Manjula the opportunity to show that she is aware of important things during the visit. Sitting in her wheelchair, beneath the cathedral's Rose Window, Manjula is left for a few minutes to look, listen, and feel where she is. As the sun shines through the window, Manjula smiles and wrings her hands with pleasure. Back in school, Manjula's teacher and learning support assistant help her to make a 'sensory' picture book as part of a topic on the cathedral. They make her a personal tape of the kind of organ music heard during the visit. This brings learning to life for Manjula, and brings other real benefits. Some of her classmates also enjoy the organ music and the class teacher organises a small 'listening group'. Manjula's mother and father, when they hear about this successful activity, decide to make her a tape of Buddhist chants used in their community temple. Thereafter, whenever the family visits the temple, they play the tape in the car and Manjula gets very excited with anticipation. The curriculum experience described here has been well matched to Manjula's needs, and importantly, this has been 'negotiated' on the basis of her response to an activity. She might have been left out of the school visit, but instead she was included and showed her educators, friends and family that she was developing a seemingly new awareness that could help her develop valuable choice making skills.

In fact, Manjula's teacher, Ms Hunter, surprised by the extent of her awareness, decided that she should try to identify more opportunities to facilitate active participation and involvement in lessons. This involved looking at different curriculum subjects, with a view to ensuring that Manjula could join in fully. Manjula's designated learning support assistant was also involved in this planning and made some additional resources ('feely books', story and music tapes) to provide 'concrete' learning experiences.

This example has focused on the complex educational needs of a pupil with profound and multiple learning difficulties. The kind of sensitive thinking and planning of the kind outlined is equally important for all pupils with learning difficulties, and should always be looking towards making the curriculum meaningful. Meaningful learning will provide pupils with interesting – and sometimes novel – experiences, some of which cannot be anticipated. These experiences need to be built upon, often in a structured way that provides opportunities for more partially supported and independent participation and involvement. When this is evident it becomes easier to plan the next steps in learning, and to identify the most appropriate curriculum activities.

If this kind of teaching and assessment clarification is not carried out, then many pupils with learning difficulties may well be **present** in mainstream classes, but not learn optimally. Fortunately, there is a growing body of evidence to suggest that such practice is developing, and this is exemplified in the educational experience of Marie described in Chapter 1. At its best, this practice adheres to principles outlined in the *Code of Practice* (Department for Education 1994: 1:2) which place the pupil at the centre of the assessment and provision process. Adherence to these principles requires flexibility at school level in the interpretation of curriculum and assessment guidance (Department for Education and Employment 1997).

As Byers and Rose (1996) note, it is possible for schools to undertake curriculum development that, as well as complying with statutory regulations, is creative and reflective of the needs of their pupils. It is all too easy to forget that flexibility is allowed. A useful way of thinking about flexible provision is to see it as consisting of three linked strands. Strand one is concerned with mapping curriculum entitlement for individual pupils with learning difficulties. The task here, for class or subject teachers, is to get an overall picture of a pupil's attainments across the curriculum as a whole. Strand two is concerned with identifying the strengths and needs of the individual pupil (considered in more detail later in this chapter). In doing this, it is possible to highlight what additional and extra support a pupil will need. The third and final strand involves the teacher in considering where there might be opportunities to address the needs of pupils at group, or whole-class levels. Using these strands, or dimensions of curriculum planning, teachers, working in collaboration with individual pupils, other staff and parents, can make positive and necessary decisions about provision. Less than perfect choices may have to be made, for the school day is finite. However, negotiated and informed decision-making based on discussions between everyone involved, can still lead to good optimal curriculum provision.

David is a twelve-year-old pupil who has moderate learning difficulties. He attends a local comprehensive school and is supported in his learning by three key people in addition to his subject teachers. These 'core' staff are his form teacher, one of the school's two SENCOs and a learning support assistant who works with him directly or indirectly for fifteen hours a week.

David has particular needs in the 'basic skills' associated with English and mathematics. A curriculum mapping (strand one) exercise undertaken by the SENCO is revealing. It shows that David is well regarded by all of his teachers, and that he is actually making good progress in physical education, art, music and design and technology. He experiences greater difficulties in other subjects. Closer scrutiny (strand two) reveals that he needs more substantial support in English and mathematics. Currently in these lessons he receives some additional partial support from the designated learning support assistant, but this is not having a positive impact on his attainment.

Closer observation (strand three), or auditing, reveals that David is one of a number of pupils needing to develop literacy and numeracy skills. A planning decision is therefore made, involving a range of other staff in school, a number of pupils and their parents. It is proposed that from the beginning of the new term:

- more carefully targeted learning support will be put in place during English and mathematics lessons; this support will, under the SENCO's guidance, introduce activities designed to improve self-esteem and oracy;
- this more focused and direct support will be implemented following the delivery of staff INSET designed to look at better maths resources and an approach to teaching reading called **Literacy Acceleration**;
- in David's case, his support in lessons where he is doing well will be withdrawn. He does not feel it is necessary; his subject teachers and the designated learning support assistant are less certain about this, but they agree to trial the new approach and to monitor his progress.

The changes in curriculum provision identified here are not radical, but they do include 'knock on' consequences for school organisation (staff deployment and the provision of material resources) and staff development. For David, problems of curriculum balance, breadth and relevance have been resolved. Other examples might indicate that more difficult decisions concerned with breadth and relevance have to be made. A pupil with cerebral palsy and learning difficulties might need to participate in regular physiotherapy sessions. Ideally, these sessions would be integrated into physical education lessons, but compromises might have to be made. An alternative might be to allow the pupil to visit a therapy clinic after school, or during a school option period. Decisions of this kind cannot be made lightly, but should take strong account of a pupil's views. She or he might be happy to work on therapy objectives within lessons, or prefer to keep these separate from curriculum activity.

The rest of this chapter looks more closely at the decision-making approach to the curriculum (already referred to) and outlines a framework for intervention designed to help ensure that pupils with learning difficulties can access and engage with the curriculum. The framework can be used in conjunction with the *Code of Practice*, for it implicitly addresses aspects of individual education planning. At the same time, it can be used as a more general tool to ensure that the individual needs of **all** learners are considered in mainstream classes. In a sense, it can be seen as a 'mindset' to inform planning, teaching and assessment, one premised on the positive view of pupils with learning difficulties outlined in Chapter 1.

A framework for intervention

The framework for considering needs assumes a commitment to differentiation as described by Falconer-Hall (1992):

> Differentiation is about matching what teachers want pupils to learn – the curriculum – and what pupils bring to their learning – their experiences, knowledge, skills and attitudes. It follows that assessment and differentiation are **entwined**. (p. 20, emphasis added)

It also assumes, at every stage, a consideration of the views of the learner as discussed later in Chapter 3. The framework can be summarised under the following headings, each of which will be discussed in relation to the needs of individuals and the curriculum.

Strengths and needs
Setting learning priorities
Teaching methods and strategies
Keeping track of progress
Evaluating interventions

It would though be inappropriate to use this framework, without at the same time, keeping a 'bigger picture' of curriculum entitlement in view. In practice, this means that the processes of assessment and intervention operating at the individual level need to be continually referenced to considerations of curriculum breadth and balance (strand one). Failure to do this will inevitably lead to a narrowing of educational experience and an underestimation of educational capabilities.

Strengths and needs

Before embarking on curriculum planning for individual pupils with learning difficulties it is important to map their relative strengths and needs. It is particularly useful to try and identify strengths initially, for two reasons. First, it is easy to fall into the trap of listing things a pupil 'can't do', her or his 'deficits'. An initial consideration of strengths can produce a surprisingly long list of things a pupil can do, and do well. Secondly, this listing can provide information that might be useful in addressing needs or difficulties. To reflect the interactive nature of both strengths and needs it is important too to consider aspects of a pupil's environment that impact on needs. Environmental and pupil factors that could be significant have been summarised by Wedell (1995b):

A pupil's strengths and needs:
● sensory and motor function and health
● emotional state, self-image, motivation and interests
● cognitive and intellectual function
● communication skills and competencies
● basic educational tool skills and their components
● approaches to learning
● social skills and interaction with others

Environmental factors which could lessen or contribute to needs:
● at school (appropriateness of curriculum, teaching methods and classroom management)
● in the home and family (including relationships with immediate or extended family)
● elsewhere (including links in the community)

(p. 21)

This approach to identifying strengths and needs should focus on those things relevant to improving curriculum access. At the same time, it encourages more general reflection (assessment) on factors, perhaps significant ones, that could be overlooked. The example of Suzanne illustrates this.

Suzanne, a twelve-year-old pupil with severe learning difficulties attends her local comprehensive school. It is agreed by everyone involved in her education that she is making good progress in most subjects of the curriculum, 'commensurate with her assessed abilities'. However, they are concerned about her involvement and achievement in physical education. In fact, what has been overlooked by the school, and the previous special school that Suzanne attended, is that she has motor difficulties of the kind associated with developmental coordination disorder (DCD). The difficulties have not been noticed previously, or been 'masked' by a focusing on her cognitive or learning difficulties. A 'tracking back' and examination of her early education and medical files reveals that a question was raised about her motor problems when she was four. In fact, this discovery is not simply bad news for Suzanne. Her school SENCO and the PE coordinator both know a little about DCD and are able to refer to an occupational therapist for further assessment. A result of this is the devising of an intervention programme designed to improve Suzanne's gross motor skills within PE lessons when she works with the support of a learning support assistant (LSA). Suzanne also rejoins an out-of-school swimming club that she used to attend when she was younger, and this too contributes to the development of her motor skills.

The changes made to Suzanne's curriculum provision and extra curricular activity arose directly from a careful consideration of her strengths and needs. This revealed an unforeseen difficulty that could be addressed. This example also reveals that is never too late to review pupils' strengths and needs. Indeed, it is worth doing this regularly on either a formal or informal basis.

Setting learning priorities

Having identified a pupil's strengths and needs it is appropriate to consider how these can and should be linked to learning priorities within the curriculum. Priorities are likely to be of two kinds:

1. those that are broad in scope, covering important aspects of learning that can be developed across the curriculum (e.g. increasing attention or working cooperatively);
2. those that are much more specific (e.g. within subject learning goals or skills needed in unsupervised settings such as the playground).

Learning priorities can be established in relation to either short-term (a month) or longer-term (a term, or school year) plans for learning. Once decided upon, clearer learning targets, based on these priorities, need to be identified. Since the introduction of IEP target-setting, recommended in the *Code of Practice*, much has been learned about setting too many targets for pupils, and current recommendations (DfEE 1998) suggest:

> IEPs are generally most helpful when they are crisply written, focusing on three or four short-term targets for the child, typically targets relating to key skills, such as communication skills, literacy, numeracy, behaviour and social skills (pp. 15–16).

It may be appropriate to write targets for (and with) pupils according to the popular SMART formula:

*S*pecific, *M*anageable, *A*chievable, *R*elevant and *T*imed

This approach may enable learning outcomes to be easily measured. However, as Tod, Castle and Blamires (1998) note, it may not be appropriate for **all** targets to be written in this way, and there may be good reasons for not prescribing learning in such a narrow and specific way. For example, a SMART target may focus on a very narrow aspect of learning and dwell too much on 'basics', or it may not allow for important but unintended learning outcomes. A useful way of thinking about designing educational targets for individual pupils is to view them in terms of how they help pupils to do the following:

Access learning opportunities
e.g. Victoria, a pupil with learning difficulties and associated attentional problems may need to sit in a specific place to focus on a teacher's instructions. She may also need to learn how to indicate to the teacher she needs help, or does not understand something (perhaps using a cue/symbol card to remind her when 'stuck').

Participate in the learning **process**
e.g. Devon, who has learning difficulties and a physical disability, will participate in class discussions using gesture (Makaton signs) and his Liberator communication aid.

Respond to teaching
e.g. Katie, has moderate learning difficulties, is extremely shy and reluctant to undertake any written work. When asked to carry out written tasks such as story- or letter-writing, Katie will make a short plan (using a script of points provided by her teacher) and talk this through with the class learning support assistant.

Undertake specific **curriculum** activities
e.g. In a series of orienteering lessons (geography and physical education) Ally, who has severe learning difficulties will make a map of the course set out in the school playground. She will use the map to navigate the course without help.

Improve skills in **personal development**
e.g. Mark, a pupil with profound and multiple learning difficulties, will participate in certain lessons without direct learning support assistance.

These examples focus on pupils, but target-setting could also describe the activities of teachers and learning support assistants, identifying how best they can meet a pupil's needs. Good target-setting should provide positive answers to the following questions:

- Do the targets set really address identified concerns and priorities, that which is 'additional and extra'?
- Do they provide challenges for the pupil?
- Do they avoid isolating and excluding the pupil?
- Do they clarify what needs to be taught (rather than make it more complex)?
- Are they easily understood by everyone involved?

- To what extent has the design of targets involved all concerned (e.g. pupil, parent, learning support assistant)?
- Do targets provide a focus and means for curriculum and staff development?

(adapted from Tod *et al.* 1998: 44)

These questions are really concerned with trying to make sure that target-setting does not become an end in itself, or an act of compliance solely to satisfy the requirements of auditing, or inspection. Put more positively, they are designed to try and make sure that targets are **educational**, and **embedded** in the curriculum.

Targets should also be considered carefully in relation to our understanding of pupil needs. Pupils with learning difficulties (and other pupils) have a range of needs, and understanding this can help us to consider all of them. In Chapter 1, it was shown that Adrian, Marie and Mabel – all pupils or students described as having 'special educational needs' – actually have an array of needs that are not simply reducible to the term 'SEN'. In fact, their needs are more appropriately described in the following way:

Individual needs – arising from characteristics different from all others;
Exceptional needs – arising from characteristics shared by some others;
Common needs – arising from characteristics shared by all.

(Norwich 1996: 103)

If this approach to needs is kept in view, then target-setting for pupils with learning difficulties can be undertaken in an appropriately balanced way. For example, it will be necessary to identify targets that are unique to an individual. It will also probably be appropriate to identify targets that can be addressed through particular groupings of pupils, the use of specific teaching approaches, or differentiated curriculum content. Finally, it may be appropriate to ensure that some targets are addressed in the context of teaching and learning activities designed to include all pupils. The all-important **balancing** is concerned with comprehensively addressing a pupil's full range of needs and not just those of one kind.

There is increasing evidence to show that this expansive consideration of pupil needs helps to focus on important areas of learning for pupils with learning difficulties. Two examples illustrate this. First, Watson (1999) has highlighted the benefits for these pupils of targeted teaching focused on working in groups. Her research findings showed that:

- All pupils with learning difficulties benefited from working in groups (not just the most able pupils).
- Pupils working together in groups over a period of time spoke for longer, had more extended conversations with each other and engaged in more interactions.
- All of the pupils involved absorbed information and showed gains in confidence.

- The pupils also showed improved emotional engagement and increased social awareness.
- Pupil-to-pupil conversations emerged, decreasing dependency on teacher led communication.

(p. 94)

Target-setting, in the context of this evidence, clearly ought to enable the identification of opportunities within curriculum provision for shared and common needs to be addressed.

A second example, shows how inclusive educational practice can be fostered when individual needs are considered in the context of **whole** class teaching and learning. Research by Salisbury *et al.* (1995) mapped features of the inclusive education process and identified discernible themes of good or **welcoming** practice, including:

- Teachers actively planning **social interaction** between **all** pupils.
- Interaction carefully **targeted** within **cooperative** and **collaborative** activities.
- Pupils **caring** and taking **responsibility** for each other.
- Pupils **modelling acceptance** of each other.

(p. 134)

These themes were also supported by wider aspects of school organisation and policy. Again, what we see here, is the idea of targeted teaching being located in the social activity of classrooms and schools, within which consideration is given to individual pupils. A more detailed discussion of this kind of approach and ideas for putting it into practice follow in Part II (Chapter 4).

A final but important observation to make about the setting of learning priorities is that the process should, together with the curriculum itself be 'framed' within a set of overarching and long-term aims. These aims should focus upon a preparation for adulthood (Griffiths 1994) of the kind that fosters:

1. the achievement of personal autonomy;
2. productive activity (including employment);
3. social interaction and community participation;
4. roles and relationships within partnership, families and friendship groups.

Progress towards these aims can begin within early years and primary school provision, and continue with greater specificity as pupils enter secondary schooling.

Teaching methods and strategies

Having identified educational priorities and targets, it is necessary to consider **how** to teach aspects of the curriculum that we want pupils to learn, and **what** strategies to use. This most important part of the framework for intervention is discussed in detail in Part II. At this point it is simply worth highlighting a significant quantitative and qualitative distinction in the use of teaching methods and strategies. On the one hand, it may be entirely appropriate to meet the needs of a pupil with learning difficulties by allowing more time and practice (quantity). Specialist teaching approaches are not required, but 'ordinary' ones need to be applied with greater intensity. On the other hand, the particular needs of an individual pupil, or a group of pupils, may be best met through the use of teaching approaches which reflect a knowledge, often based on some research evidence, of 'what works best' (quality). This distinction in approaches is helpful for decision-making concerned with teaching and learning, but it is of course possible to use both ordinary and more specialist methods together.

Keeping track of progress

Having established learning priorities, identified learning targets and started teaching a pupil using carefully considered methods and strategies, it is important to make sense of progress being made. To do this, some kind of record needs to be kept for the following reasons.

First, it is important to consider whether or not a pupil is making progress, and at a rate that is appropriate.

Secondly, recorded evidence of teaching and learning enables adjustments to be made to the teaching process. Here, it worth noting that difficulties in learning experienced by a pupil may arise because one part of a teaching sequence is creating problems. If this can be identified, then successful learning may resume. This kind of formative assessment, is essential if pupils with learning difficulties are not to become 'helpless' learners (Sylva 1994).

Thirdly, recording and assessment should communicate progress to the pupil. This may entail presenting information in an accessible way (e.g. the use of pictures or symbols), but it should also involve frequent conversations about progress made, so that pupils can report their learning experiences (Rose, McNamara and O'Neill 1996). These can be short and informal, but they need to be frequent. Of course, feedback of this kind can be a feature of work with all pupils, and this is something incorporated into good practice associated with both the national literacy and numeracy strategies.

Fourthly, recording and assessment needs to be communicative with other people involved in a pupil's education, and this will include parents (Blamires *et al.* 1997) and learning support staff (Fox 1998).

These four essentials of tracking progress at the individual pupil level need to be supported by wider school practice in assessment that strives to ensure full curriculum access for pupils with learning difficulties. Some key questions to ask about the process of assessment have been identified by Cline (1992), and grouped under the following four headings (principles).

Theoretical Integrity
− Is it based on an acceptable model of disabilities and learning difficulties?
− Does its implicit model of personality development incorporate all aspects of development, and is it based on an acceptable model of the learning process that respects the autonomy and initiative of the learner?
− Does it explicitly focus on aspects that are necessary for successful learning?
− Does the process of assessment and the information it yields tend to foster inclusion?

Practical Efficacy
− Does it draw upon the richest sources of information available?
− Does it produce information that can lead directly to improvements in teaching and learning?
− Does the way the assessment is conducted empower children, parents and teachers?

Equity
− Are the rights of children and parents effectively protected?
− Does the process operate without bias with respect to gender, social class, ethnicity, language use and religion?

Accountability
− Is the process and the information it produces open and intelligible to children, parents, teachers, other professionals, the education authority?
− Is the process cost effective?

(adapted from Cline 1992: 122–3)

The application of some of these questions and their underlying principles can be seen in the following example.

Tomas, a seven-year-old pupil who attends a local primary school, is considered to have significant learning and behavioural difficulties. His poor attention span and high levels of activity have caused staff in the school to ask whether he might have a specific difficulty, perhaps of the kind associated with Attention Deficit and Hyperactivity Disorder (ADHD). However, problems of attention and high levels of activity should not necessarily lead to 'labelling' which can be stigmatising.

Careful assessment of Tomas is needed. His 'behavioural difficulties' and 'ADHD' could easily mask a consideration of his perhaps considerable learning needs. His initiative and autonomy, currently expressed in high levels of active play, could be 'read' as an abnormal symptom, to be tackled by implementing a carefully structured programme. An alternative interpretation might recognise his delayed physical and cognitive maturation, and identify a need for frequent free and semi-structured play. Assessment could also discover how much he enjoys exploratory play in a local park, that he adores going on 'daring rides' during holiday visits to a theme park and can name at least twelve of these and draw them.

A lot of time and energy could be spent on assessing Tomas' needs out of context, perhaps at various clinic appointments in different places. It might be much more informative and effective for this effort to be focused on learning about his activity in school, at home and in the community.

This example is not presented to dismiss a diagnosis of ADHD, but to highlight the importance of working with assessment principles that encourage reflection, rigour and sensitivity. Without adherence to such principles, pupils with learning difficulties are unlikely to have their needs either fully or fairly assessed. As more pupils with severe and profound and multiple learning difficulties begin to attend mainstream schools further attention may also need to be given to assessment, to ensure that it genuinely enhances and reflects their progress. Teachers taking prime responsibility for these pupils will need to have opportunities to undertake further continuing professional development that addresses issues of curriculum content and the assessment of learning for pupils with profound and multiple learning difficulties.

Evaluating interventions

In addition to the continuous assessment of targeted learning, a summative evaluation of progress is also needed. This needs to reflect back on agreed learning priorities and their associated targets, or goals. This evaluation should be at various levels, reflecting the ecology of teaching and learning:

1. It should review a pupil's progress over the mid to long-term (and may be linked to an Annual Review for a pupil with a Statement of Special Educational Needs).
2. It should look at aspects of the teaching and learning environment, with a view to making changes needed. For example, classroom layout or grouping for certain activities may warrant modification. This review of context will also require a teacher to reflect on her or his approach to teaching particular pupils. To this end, it will be helpful for the teacher to get feedback from pupils themselves.
3. Wider aspects of school or department organisation may be appropriate to examine. For example, dining-room or playground arrangements may need adapting or a school-wide approach to teaching may need altering.

These levels of review and evaluation are interlinked, and though they have been outlined with individual teacher–pupil relations in mind, they can also be used to gather useful information about groups of pupils experiencing difficulties. This information can help identify areas for curriculum change and staff development.

For example, scrutiny of pupil progress may reveal that teachers working with pupils who have learning difficulties do not have adequate curriculum resource material for the teaching of reading, science, or physical education. Once shortfalls in curriculum provision or resources have been clearly identified then a school as a whole can set about redressing the problem.

The five aspects of the framework for intervention described here: identifying strengths and needs, setting learning priorities, using carefully thought out teaching methods and strategies, keeping track of progress, and evaluating interventions, if put into practice should contribute to ensuring that pupils with learning difficulties are included fully in mainstream educational settings. The overall approach outlined is one premised on the view that pupils with learning difficulties are not different from other children. However, if their needs are to be fully met, then all aspects of teaching need, as Wright and Sugden (1999: 27) note, to be 'specified in some detail, with the teaching process being based on the resources of the child, the tasks to be learned, and the context in which learning takes place'. Only through such detailed planning can the curriculum be fully engaged with.

Conclusion

In this chapter we have considered some ways of ensuring that pupils with learning difficulties can fully access the curriculum. A framework to help facilitate this access has been outlined. Part II looks more closely at this framework in action. Effectively meeting the needs of pupils with learning difficulties places a lot of responsibilities on the class or subject teacher, and these should not be underestimated. However, she or he should expect to be supported in meeting the needs of pupils with learning difficulties by a range of other colleagues, and by the SENCO in particular. The sensitive, supportive school, successful in including all learners, will also be one that has an active special educational needs, or inclusion policy (Beveridge 1996). This policy will be reflected in how the school as a whole is organised to support learning. Part II provides practical advice on how collaborative support at various levels can help schools to be responsive to the needs of pupils and at the same time be educationally effective.

Part II Classroom Practice

In the second part of this book, the rationale and the framework that have been presented in the first part will be expanded in a classroom context. Examples will be used to illustrate the points being made and these will span the range of ability across learning difficulties. The emphasis will be on the learning process and the ways in which pupils, including those with learning difficulties, can be encouraged to be more effective learners and thinkers.

Chapter 3 is focused on identification of needs and the importance of being clear about these needs in the process of becoming an effective learner. In Chapter 4, thinking and learning are explored in terms of learning style and the kinds of strategies that pupils can use to become more effective learners. Chapter 5 is devoted to what teachers can do to encourage this effective learning and Chapter 6 to the kind of environment that schools need to provide for its success to be likely.

The examples in this section are drawn from the good practice that we have been involved in or seen in this country. The pupils and their teachers are all anonymous but the practice illustrated is real. We are tempted to add: 'If it can happen somewhere, it can happen everywhere.'

CHAPTER 3

Identifying learning needs

In this chapter aspects of identifying learning needs will be discussed, particularly focusing on:

- identification and assessment of needs;
- pupil involvement in identifying their own needs;
- ensuring that the needs identified really relate to the pupil;
- preventing learning difficulties.

Identification and assessment of needs

Most pupils with severe and profound learning difficulties will have experienced a thorough identification and assessment procedure before they reach the mainstream reception class, although children with SEN can join schools at any age (perhaps from a special school). Those with more severe needs are likely to have been to a child development centre or assessment nursery where they will have been observed and tested, the results of which should be available to class teachers, following the process of writing a statement of special educational needs (SEN). Pupils with more moderate or mild learning difficulties are likely to be in school for some time before their needs become evident. They will probably be assessed, work according to an Individual Education Plan (IEP) and perhaps have a statement of SEN.

As stressed in the first chapter, it can be argued that many of these learning difficulties can actually be created by schools, by the type of curriculum there is on offer and by the approaches there are to teaching and learning and that if these were changed, difficulties in learning would disappear or at least be reduced. A truly inclusive school should be able to meet the needs of the widest range of pupils, providing experiences which encourage learning appropriate to level of development related to speed and style of learning.

If that argument is accepted, then assessment is not about identifying special educational needs. It is a process through which teachers (and others who work in schools) can identify individual pupil levels of development, their strengths and needs, their interests, their favoured learning style, their responses to teaching styles, their optimum learning environment and the support they need in order to be able to learn most effectively. It is a dynamic process: one which is sensitive to changes and capable of picking up potential for learning rather than seeking out specific difficulties.

There are many assessment tools that can help identify pupil learning needs, far too many to be listed here. Some such tools merely compare the individual pupil's level of functioning with a so-called 'norm'. These tests rarely offer any help with identifying the actual learning needs of the pupil. Other kinds of assessments are more helpful to the learning process as they show where pupils are making mistakes and enable analysis of the way in which they are learning. So when seeking an assessment that will help in this analysis, look for a tool that:

- enables analysis of the **processes** of learning, not just the **product**, and
- offers teaching advice as well as diagnosis

as these are likely to be the most useful in classroom practice.

It is also helpful to get into the habit of asking pupils **how** they are working and learning. 'How did you get that answer?' or 'Tell me what you were thinking when you wrote that?' or 'How did you remember that vocabulary?' and observing carefully what they are demonstrating through their approaches to learning. It may be necessary to rely completely on observation with pupils who are not able to articulate what they are doing.

Pupil involvement

Traditionally, assessment and identification of needs are wholly in the hands of the assessor who administers tests which are designed to show the difference between what is considered usual for a child's age or developmental stage and what is considered unusual. For example, a reading age is calculated in relation to what is 'normally' expected; motor ability is measured against a scale of 'normal' development; and National Curriculum Level is rated against descriptions based on learning levels expected of 'normal' children. Saying someone has Special Educational Needs is the result of measurements which demonstrate the child has failed to reach the levels designated 'normal'.

Pupils themselves have little role to play in the traditional perspective on assessment. It is something that is done to them. In a dynamic view of assessment, pupils have a central part to play. They are involved in identifying their own needs and in planning how they will be met, setting their own targets and monitoring their own progress. There are several frameworks that can support pupil involvement, such as records of achievement (Hardwick and Rushton 1994) and 'plan–do–review' sequences (Hohmann and Weikhart 1995) but it is also possible to use IEPs and target-setting in an interactive way, with pupils helping to set their own targets and plotting the route towards achieving them.

Pupils with learning difficulties need support to be able to participate in the process of identifying their learning needs and setting realistic targets. They need to be taught how to make choices, predict what will happen and evaluate consequences.

Bahdria is described as having moderate learning difficulties. She is learning to set her own targets for writing. She has spent several sessions with the teacher while they get a clear picture of her strengths alongside the things she finds difficult. The teacher has a framework for teaching writing and she shows Bahdria where she fits into the early part of this framework. Together they decide what Bahdria should be learning next and they write the short-term targets using the computer programme, Writing with Symbols. At the review of her IEP, Bahdria and her teacher discuss the programme they have written with the others who attend the meeting.

Following this meeting, the short-term targets are adjusted and Bahdria works on them for the next few weeks. During these weeks, Bahdria learns how to evaluate how well she is working. She ticks off the symbols she feels she has learned and makes a record book containing the pieces of writing she feels are good. Her teacher supports her when selecting these pieces and writes brief comments after them to describe why they are good.

A few pupils with the most profound intellectual impairments will require much more support than the young person in the previous example. They will require people who can be advocates for them, interpreting little or unusual communications as indicative of needs.

As the result of several controlled observations using an assessment called 'The Affective Communication Assessment' (Coupe *et al.* 1985), Richard has been seen to raise his arm and stop moving when he appears to be enjoying an activity, particularly those activities that involve touch. The significant adults in his life begin to interpret this arm raise as an indication of approval, repeating the activity when Richard's arm is raised or waiting for it to be raised before continuing. It is not thought that Richard is deliberately communicating 'I like that' or 'more please' but sensitive adults around him are helping him to develop an intention to communicate.

Richard's IEP contains the following target: 'to use an arm raise to indicate enjoyment or request more'. Although Richard is not able to negotiate this target directly, the close observations carried out by classroom staff have enabled them to be directly guided by his needs. The target has not been arrived at through an arbitrary process of, for example finding the next target on a developmental list, but through careful observation coupled with a knowledge of early child development.

The resulting short-term targets are written with very clear directions to adults regarding how long they should wait for Richard to raise his arm or the activities to be used that are known to provoke an arm raise. He is also given activities which are known not to evoke a response to give Richard the opportunity to begin to discriminate between activities he likes and activities he does not like.

However severe their learning difficulties, pupils can be consulted during the identification of needs and the setting of learning targets, even if this is essentially through a proxy. Becoming familiar with your own strengths and needs can help considerably in making progress, especially if this is coupled with a clear path forward.

Whose needs?

There is a message from the previous section (on pupil involvement) which relates to being clear about whose needs are being met through setting targets. It is easy to get confused about the cause of pupils' difficulties and about the best way to help them. The child who disrupts lessons, wasting time and distracting others could be reacting to many different things in his or her life. There may be a family crisis, or the child may be seeking attention that he or she does not get elsewhere, or he or she may be distracting attention away from the struggle to read, or may find it impossible to concentrate when others are visible. There are many alternatives. It is important to get clear the cause of the difficulty and identify the actual need before rushing into a programme to change behaviour. It may be the teacher's 'need' to get the child to sit quietly and carry out given tasks but it may not be the child's.

Maria always chooses to sit at the back of the class, where she spends most lessons doodling in her rough book and talking to the people she is sitting next to. During whole-class sessions, she wriggles constantly and never puts up her hand. When asked a direct question she usually says something which would amuse the rest of the class and disrupt the flow. In writing exercises, Maria rarely writes more than a few sentences and she spends most of the time preventing others from writing too.

Mr Long, the teacher, tries the usual tactics of asking her to behave, then ignoring the behaviour coupled with lots of positive encouragement but as neither works for long, he decides he has to investigate further. What is the cause of the disruptive behaviour? First, Mr Long talked to others who worked with Maria and together they build up a picture of her behaviour and of her learning from their point of view. Then he observes her in class more closely to see if he can understand what is happening. He also looks at all the records available on her progress and speaks to her parents. From all these data it is clear that Maria's reading was not as far advanced as her peers, although she can read simple texts. Records on her writing show her to be a slow writer with poor formation of letters and difficulties with spelling and with making her writing relevant. She consistently scores well in speaking and listening, although there are many comments from teachers on inappropriate replies to class questioning attributed to her enjoyment of disruption. All the reports show Maria to be at the lower end of achievement in comparison with the rest of the class.

Mr Long then interviews Maria to find out her point of view. Maria talks a lot about hating writing and about her pen never being a good one, people distracting her when writing or never knowing what to write. After much probing, it appeared that what Maria finds most difficult is identifying what she has to do from what is said to the whole class. She thinks she is stupid because everyone else knows what to do but she doesn't, so she wastes time until she gets some clues and then it is often too late to write very much. She never knows what to say when asked a question because she hasn't really followed what had been said before. She can cope better when pictures or diagrams are used but when it is just words, she doesn't like it.

Between them, Mr Long and Maria work out Maria's needs. She needs people to speak specifically to her when directions are being given. She needs to be given pictures and diagrams to accompany words and, long-term, she needs to learn how to extract information from a busy spoken-word environment. From the expression of these needs, the two of them write an IEP to meet them, some of the detail of which referred to what the teacher should provide as well as to the learning Maria would achieve.

Had the teacher persisted with meeting his own needs, that is for a child who did not disrupt, he might never have identified that child's needs, which were to learn to respond to spoken communications in a busy setting.

Prevention of learning difficulties

The last two examples provide suggestions about how learning difficulties can actually be prevented by the actions of teachers and others. Some of Maria's difficulties can be avoided through making sure she has visual clues to help her understand what is being said and some of Richard's communication needs can be met through adults observing and interpreting his behaviour. What is most important, in both cases, is the process through which Maria and Richard's teachers have been able to find out exactly **what** and **how** their pupils are learning.

When identifying need, it is important to find what Vygotsky calls 'the zone of proximal (or next) development' (Wood 1998). This process implies assessing current independent achievement in the light of what can be achieved next, with support. Vygotsky suggests that if teaching takes place within the zone between independent and supported achievement, success should be assured. So the difficulties in learning have been translated into finding the right point to place the teaching to encourage the next learning step to take place. The key is thorough assessment of the two points to locate the zone in between, alongside an analysis of the support that is necessary to achieve the far end of the zone. This kind of assessment is called 'dynamic assessment' to denote that it is different from the 'static' assessment of what pupils can and cannot do. 'Cannot do' is of little importance. 'Can do' and 'can almost do' are.

Alongside the pupils' achievements is a thorough examination of the ways in which they are learning and thinking. What are their preferences for the way in which activities and materials are presented to them? Do they learn best through listening, through looking, through touching? How can teachers find out so that they teach in the optimum way and thus go some way actually to prevent learning difficulties from occurring? The topic of the next chapter, cognitive and learning styles, can be a useful place to begin to understand and plan for pupils to learn most effectively.

Conclusion

Traditionally, assessment of pupils with learning difficulties has been related to diagonosing these difficulties through locating them within patterns of so-called 'normal' learning. It has been argued, in this chapter, that his traditional approach is less helpful than a more 'dynamic' view of children difficulties based on an assessment of pupil strengths and needs. Teachers' observations are at the centre of an assessment process that is aimed at preventing the difficulties from interfering with learning. We are not arguing that learning difficulties do not exist but that if asssessment really does identify fundamentals about needs, then teaching and learning can be tailored to these needs and children can learn at their own pace and level.

This sounds like an ideal world, where each individual children's needs can be identified and met: where there are endless adults on hand to provide individual attention. Obviously every child's individual need cannot be constantly in mind in a class of thirty children with one or maybe two adults. However, if the individual with learning difficulties is not constantly going to fail at unsuitable tasks, the ideal must be striven for where possible. Sometimes, as was seen in the example of Maria, observing and investigating carefully can reveal a difficulty that can quite easily be met in the short-term, although there are long-term implications for teaching Maria how to learn in the busy verbal environment found in schools.

It may be that some of Maria's needs are shared with others in her class. As will be seen in the next chapter, there are preferred learning styles that are identifiable in groups of pupils. So, for example, there will be other pupils in Maria's class who prefer to learn through pictures and diagrams. They may be capable of learning through language more effectively than Maria but providing opportunities for learning through visual means will serve the needs of more than just one child with 'so-called' special educational needs.

CHAPTER 4

Learning styles and learning how to learn

In this chapter, several aspects of effective learning will be explored. Pupils with learning difficulties are still at the centre of the discussion but their needs will be seen in relation to the needs of all learners. The stance taken in this book is that, although some pupils may find learning difficult, they are likely to learn effectively in social rather than isolated situations. They may have individual needs but these can be met through working with others (peers and adults) in supportive environments.

Topics covered in this chapter are:

- learning styles
- learning how to learn
- motivation
- memory strategies
- cognitive mapping
- problem-solving

These topics relate to the fundamental processes of learning and underpin the whole curriculum.

Learning styles

Results of research into cognitive style by, for example Riding and Rayner (1998) suggest that everyone has a preferred style of thinking and learning. One dimension to this style can be plotted on a continuum between those who tend to process information as a whole (wholists) and those who prefer to see the parts (analysts). The other dimension is a continuum between those who think in language (verbalisers) and those who use mental pictures (imagers). In Figure 4.1 the vertical line represents the continuum between verbalisers (top) and imagers (bottom) and the horizontal, between wholists (left) and analysts (right). Placing the dimensions in this way indicate four major learning-style groups, although many learners will not fall neatly into one of the four.

| wholist-verbaliser | analytic-verbaliser |
| wholist-imager | analytic-imager |

Figure 4.1   Four major learning-style groups

In broad terms the practical application of this research points to the necessity for teachers to expect that pupils in their classes will learn in different ways and to plan accordingly. Thus, they use both texts and images and give opportunities for step-by-step tasks as well as large-scale overviews. [There are a number of assessment tools that help teachers identify their pupils' preferred learning style, for example, 'The Learning Style Profile' (Keefe 1989)].

Matching every pupils' learning objectives to his or her preferred learning style all the time is not possible (nor desirable as one general learning objective should be that pupils **learn to learn** in different ways) but recognising that there needs to be a variety of ways of accessing skills, knowledge and understanding can be a useful tool for preventing difficulties in learning (Reid 1998). If a pupil who prefers to learn through a tight structure with facts to memorise is constantly exposed to a loose structure with opportunities for discovering principles, she or he will not learn easily. Not only will this pupil need lessons organised in the preferred style but he or she will also need temporary structures which are gradually faded alongside clear support towards grasping principles.

Ling has severe learning difficulties but he has good verbal skills. It is easy to believe that Ling understands everything he says and hears, but this is not so. Careful listening to his language reveals much repetition, stock phrases and constant changing of the subject from something he does not understand to something with which he can engage. Ling has particular difficulty with questions other than those which require him to name something such as 'what day is it today?' or 'which day do you go swimming?' Ling enjoys working with other pupils, although he does tend to use his verbal skills to divert from producing written or practical work.

Contrary to first impressions, Ling does not learn best through language. He responds best to pictures and symbols which give him more time to understand what is going on than words can. Ling finds it difficult to grasp the whole activity and responds better when he is given a specific task to do. When cooking, Ling can succeed if he has a card with a symbol to represent each step which he follows through carefully. He is learning to recall these steps after the activity, using the cards as prompts. He is also practising answering questions using cards and photographs to aid his thinking.

Another way of capitalising on knowledge about learning styles is through sometimes grouping pupils together to obtain complementary styles for co-operative activities (see Chapter 6) and, at other times, grouping those with similar styles together to use similar materials. Putting together wholists with analysts can be very effective when the outcome to the activity is open-ended.

Four pupils are working together on class rules. Paul is strongly a wholist-imager and Spencer is definitely an analytic-verbaliser but Anatol and Mark are both somewhere near the middle of the continuum in their learning styles, Mark leaning towards wholist-imager and Anatol towards wholist-verbaliser. Mark has learning difficulties and is the least able in the group. He depends on the others for direction, although he can contribute thoughtful ideas when given time to speak. Spencer usually prefers to work on his own, but is prepared to lead the group, making sure everyone has a chance to say something. During the discussion, he gets involved in the detail of different rules and forgets the direction of whole task, but Paul reminds them all of what they are supposed to be doing and keeps an eye on the clock. Anatol sometimes dominates the group but his good verbal memory means that he is the natural person to present the work of the group. Mark is pulled along by the others and contributes when he is asked.

Groups such as these have been specifically taught how to work together. They have practised listening to each other in turn, discussing a topic and coming up with ideas and they have learned a little about the different ways in which they like to learn.

Learning how to learn

Learning something about your own learning style can be helpful when trying to improve the way in which you learn and think. Learning how to learn and think is important for everyone, but is particularly significant for those who find learning difficult. Analysing how learning occurs can be very helpful when developing the skills. How do you remember a telephone number? Do you divide it into twos or threes? Do you have a mental picture of the numerals? Do you associate it with a date? Do you make sums with it? Do you put it into a story? I have actually done all of these things depending on the number to be remembered. Few people with learning difficulties would use any of these strategies unless they were taught to.

Some learning strategies are easier to teach than others. Asking questions, planning and monitoring what you have done are relatively easy to teach (Babbage et al. 1999), although, for some pupils with learning difficulties they can present enormous barriers to learning. Answering questions other than those that require data recollection, such as naming objects or actions, can be very challenging to some pupils and asking questions other than the trivial can be even more difficult. In the early 1980s, the staff at Rectory Paddock School (1982) were deliberately teaching pupils with severe learning difficulties how to answer questions that involved them in more complex thought such as speculation, hypothesis generation, reasoning, analysis, evaluation or problem-solving (Kerry 1982). They were also teaching pupils how to discriminate between questions they could answer, such as 'is it raining today?' and those they could not such as 'will it rain tomorrow?'

Teaching pupils with learning difficulties to use questioning as a learning strategy is complex, but important. Experienced learners use this strategy constantly although the questions may only be half-formed and the learner may not be aware that he or she is using them. Some are self-regulatory such as 'what shall I do next?' or 'which book shall I look that up in?' and some are aimed at gaining knowledge or understanding such as 'what kind of shoes did they wear in Tudor times?' or 'why did that chemical react in that way?' Teachers and other pupils can demonstrate questioning strategies and they can be taught specifically.

Paul has learning difficulties and does not appear to use questioning spontaneously as a learning strategy. He has difficulty in answering questions which require him to reason or analyse, such as 'Why did the man hide from the lion?' or 'Why did that car need more petrol?' The only questions he has been heard to use relate directly to him and are seen as 'comfort' questions, such as 'Are we going home now?' or 'When's dinnertime?'

The teacher works with Paul on developing his questioning techniques. She uses activities and pictures to ask him 'why' questions and encourages him to take a turn at asking her 'why' questions. She also demonstrates other types of questions, such as, when opening a book, 'Now where will I find the beginning of this story? Oh yes after the title page' and 'Who was it who wore that red hat? Ah it was this man.'

She also invites other members of the class to do some of their own questioning out loud. In whole-class sessions they are encouraged to say things like 'Where will I find out about x?' or 'I think I'll start looking for x by ...' in outer expression of an inner dialogue.

Everyone is expected to plan out loud and the teacher asks questions which enable them to achieve this, questions such as 'What are you going to do first?' or 'How much do you think you will achieve by the end of the lesson?' Questioning is transparent and is clearly about ways of learning.

As the weeks progress, Paul begins to join in and although he is still not asking questions himself, he is able to answer some questions that require thinking and reasoning. The teacher is hopeful that he will make sufficient progress to be able to use questioning to help him to plan what he is going to do.

It was suggested earlier in this chapter that questioning was relatively easy to teach, that is in comparison with learning strategies such as monitoring your own learning, checking that you have completed what you were asked to learn and self-testing, such as closing the book and trying to remember the list of spellings. It should, however, be possible to teach those through demonstration and as a response to direct questioning as in the last example. Pupils, that is all pupils, are likely to benefit from an emphasis on learning how to learn. If, routinely, they are given the opportunity to:

- define the tasks they will undertake,
- specify the outcomes from those tasks,
- set goals in terms of time, quality and quantity, and
- assess the work completed,

it is likely that they will develop good learning habits, and be less likely to waste time sharpening pencils to avoid doing work which they do not know how to tackle and in which they see little relevance. They will be more in control of their own learning (Hastings 1996).

Motivation

One aspect of learning to learn is motivation. We all know how quickly we can get on with a task and how easy it is to learn when we are well-motivated, usually intrinsically through the interest-value and satisfaction of the task itself. Learners do like to please their teachers but the strongest motivation to learn anything is because you want to. Intrinsic motivation is very difficult to teach or to change.

Some children appear to find learning difficult because they dare not take risks with it. They view learning in terms of maintaining their own self-worth and are fearful of tackling tasks which (they think) might make them look stupid. In fact, they would rather not attempt the task at all, as at least they can say that they did not achieve because they did not try. If they put in a lot of effort, regardless of the difficulty of the task, then it must prove that they are stupid. Self-worth preservers not only view failure as proving their stupidity but attribute both failure and success to factors outside of themselves, such as luck.

Hastings (1996) suggests that to help pupils who appear not to be motivated to put effort into learning, teachers should:

- ensure pupils know the purpose of the tasks they are undertaking;
- give them as much control of activities and learning as possible;
- reward learning rather an achievement;
- use collaborative groupwork to encourage a high level of engagement;
- use evaluation that focuses on the learning process and is unrelated to competition;
- with pupils, set time limits for tasks so that their completion is clear and possible.

Although it was indicated earlier that well-motivated learners do not learn in order to earn praise from their teachers, feedback (which might include praise) is clearly very important. Pupils need to know how well they are progressing in their learning but this must be clearly related to the task in hand and include the opinions of both teacher and learner. Part of learning how to learn includes being able to give yourself feedback, often guided or coached by a more experienced person, such as a teacher (Fisher 1995).

The old saying 'success breeds success' is, of course, very true in the classroom. Pupils, whether or not they have difficulties in learning, will be more likely to be effortful in their learning if they have experienced success previously. Deliberate teaching of the strategies that promote learning can contribute to this success because they are generalisable across activities. Teaching the strategies out of context, though, can lead to difficulties in generalisation; thus it is important to embed learning to learn within everything that happens in the classroom.

Mr Lucas had routines in his classroom. Some of them were verbally recalled whenever an activity was planned or reviewed and others were written out and put up on the display board for pupils to refer to.

At the start of each activity, Mr Lucas says, 'What do we have to do first?' and pupils reply 'Plan what we are going to do' or 'Read the question' or 'Choose a partner', whichever is the first step. His next question depends on the activity, but might be 'What do you need to use?' or 'How long do you think it will take you?' or 'What do you think you are going to learn?' All the time he is coaching pupils to plan their learning and keep control over it.

When he talks to pupils about their work, he says 'I like what you have done. Do you know why?' or 'Can you tell me two things that are good about this piece of work?' He gives positive feedback with remarks such as 'I like the way you used two different methods to find the answer', being very clear about what he valued in the learning process.

One of the charts on the wall contains children's illustrations of the sequence:

1. look
2. cover
3. think
4. write
5. check

and Mr Lucas periodically reminds pupils to use the strategy to help them focus, act, monitor and evaluate what they are doing.

Another chart on the wall reminds pupils how to learn best from discussions:

- Talk to each other.
- Listen to each other.
- Respond to what each other says.
- Put forward more than one point of view on the topic.
- Decide what you are going to do/say following the discussion.

There are symbols accompanying the advice so that all pupils can read it.

Memory strategies

Carefully constructed charts on the wall are useful for helping pupils who have learning difficulties as they act as memory joggers. Memory difficulties often accompany learning difficulties, especially for those with severe learning difficulties, who have particular problems with short-term memory. School education is dominated by language-based teaching and often demands that children make sense of information through recalling language. Most young children prefer to use visual memory rather than language and they do not make much use of deliberate strategies such as rehearsal or grouping until they are around seven years of age. However they do seem to benefit from being taught how to, for example, repeat a sequence of letters in their heads to help remember how to spell a word (Bristow, Cowley and Daines 1999).

Memory processes are often broken down into three stages:

1. input (attending, using the senses, taking in information);
2. storage (short and long-term memory stores, what you do with the information to remember it);
3. output (recalling the information).

Learners can experience difficulties at any or all of these three stages and difficulty at one stage can affect the others. However, difficulties of one kind, for example verbal memory, do not necessarily mean that visual or kinaesthetic (movement) memory are equally impaired. It is important to ensure that:

1. pupils are aware of and encouraged to make best use of their strengths;
2. teaching includes opportunities to use pupils' strengths.

Teachers and learners can work together to improve memory use through a range of strategies. For example:

Input
● minimise distractions;
● make sure the listener is looking at the speaker;
● encourage asking for repetition when distracted (with no blame attached);
● simplify instructions and information wherever possible and keep reminders displayed;
● highlight the most important part of the information;
● check that instructions/information have been taken in;
● use multimedia for input (being careful not to overload with information).

Storage
- check meaning in what was said and shown to the learner;
- encourage verbal rehearsing of instructions or information;
- encourage visualising what is being said or even drawing symbols as personal reminder;
- give thinking time;
- give frequent breaks, go back on what was learned and then refocus attention before each new step;
- keep focusing and refocusing on the key concepts;
- organise information for pupils (e.g. concept maps – see below).

Output
- encourage the use of substitute words and phrases for the one that cannot easily be recalled;
- use of signs and symbols in place of words;
- encourage visualising the event when it was put into the memory;
- don't be too quick to jump in – allow time for the pupil to remember;
- remind learners of strategies they have used successfully;
- provide alternatives or part of the answer as a prompt.

Memory is enormously important for learning and awareness of specific difficulties and how to improve performance should be a major aspect of education for pupils with learning difficulties.

Mrs White has pupils with a range of abilities in her class. She wants to improve the memory strategies of everyone and has allocated time within the curriculum to concentrate on this aspect of learning. First she encourages every pupil to be aware of their memories and the strategies they use to remember. She plays Kim's Game with them (a party game where objects are placed on a table and players are allowed to look at them for a short time before they are covered up and then have to be recalled). She deliberately uses objects that could be grouped together (toothbrush, soap, flannel, razor in one group and pencil, paper, rubber and paperclip in another) and then quizzes the pupils on how they remembered the objects. Those with the most developed strategies used the groupings but those with the least, did not.

From this game, Mrs White talks about other strategies such as rehearsal and visualisation and practises those with the whole class. Those with more developed skills demonstrate these to those who need to learn them and everyone becomes much more aware of possibilities. Those who use one type of strategy are encouraged to try another so everyone is learning something new. As a class they devise mnemonics for remembering frequently used spellings and how to focus the mind on a new concept. Mrs White prompts pupils to use the strategies, some of which are displayed on the wall. The strategy written out below is used for making sure that instructions have been understood and will be remembered during the activity. It is accompanied by sketches drawn by pupils. Pupils are paired with their next-door neighbour to check each other.

- Look at the speaker (two eyes).
- Open your ears (an ear).
- Check with your partner that you have heard and understood (two people talking).
- Write or draw something to remind you (drawing in book).
- Get on with your work (someone writing).
- Check that you remembered (hand pointing to drawing in book).

Mrs White has found that pupils are more thoughtful in their work and fewer misunderstand the task they are asked to do. There is also a good atmosphere among pupils as they support each other to improve their memories.

Deliberate teaching of memory strategies can be helpful to every learner, not just those who have learning difficulties. Being aware of the processes that people use to learn can equip pupils with powerful tools that can boost learning across the curriculum.

Cognitive mapping

A useful strategy for developing thinking and understanding is cognitive mapping. This is the process through which a concept such as the sea, dogs, movement, democracy can be explored, initially perhaps to find out how much you know already, then to organise your search for learning something new and then perhaps to demonstrate the results of your search. It is often presented as a spidergram or brainstorm (see Figure 4.2), although there are other ways to explore ideas, such as sequence chains, linking boxes and grouping in sets.

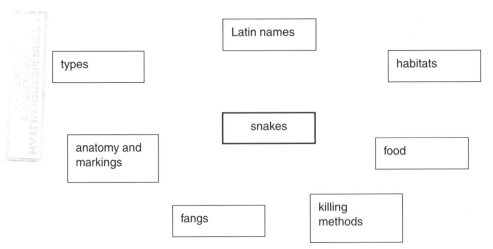

Figure 4.2   Example of cognitive mapping

Writing out what you know or have found out in this way can encourage active processing of facts and understanding. It can also be a powerful aid to memory and concept development. In themselves, concepts are ways of organising ideas that help us to understand the world, revealing patterns and frameworks and relationships. Pupils with learning difficulties often need direct illustration of the relationships between ideas, and cognitive mapping is one strategy to achieve this (Fisher 1995).

Problem-solving

The final aspect of learning how to learn that will be considered is one of the most empowering for pupils, however easy or difficult they find learning. Problem-solving is one of the fundamental objectives of education but rarely are pupils directly taught how to do it (Ashman and Conway 1993). There are generalisable principles which can be taught – although, of course, different problems demand different knowledge and understanding if they are to be successfully solved. It would be very difficult for someone to solve the problem of a spent light bulb if that person had no knowledge of electricity, however basic. Although solving the problem by finding a candle or asking someone else to help gets round the lack of knowledge.

An analysis of the process of problem-solving indicates that there are four main activities in which problem-solvers must engage:

- perception of the problem;
- thinking about the problem and its solution;
- trying out the solution;
- evaluating the success of the solution.

For those who find problem-solving difficult, there are four chances to get it wrong, but also four chances for direct teaching to help (Collis and Lacey 1996).

Many pupils with learning difficulties need support to perceive that a problem exists at all. They may be oblivious to the problem unless it is pointed out to them.

Vasilios, who has severe learning difficulties, is making a set of shelves in Technology. He selects a plane that has a very blunt blade, so blunt that it does not function. Vasilios pushes the plane backwards and forwards as he has been taught but does not notice that it is making no difference to the wood. He works for many minutes until the teacher stops him and asks him to think about what he is doing. The teacher skilfully uses questioning to direct Vasilios' attention to identifying that there is a problem, and eventually they replace the cutting blade.

Even when the problem is identified, it can be difficult for some pupils to think through the implications of the problem and then of a possible solution. Sometimes they are distracted by the need to complete the task or get involved in the minutiae of calculations or colouring that are irrelevant. Others just fail to recognise the meaning in the features of the problem, rushing in with an inappropriate solution, such as fetching paper and pencils (because that is a routine happening) when for this particular problem a card and felt-tip pens would be more useful. A more experienced problem-solver (adult or peer) can help by asking appropriate questions and providing the support needed to get the child to stop and think. This should be finely adjusted to enable the thinking to be as productive as possible. It is very tempting to jump in and solve the problem when in fact it is a golden opportunity for learning to think.

Many children who find problem-solving difficult fail to devise a plan at all. They tackle the problem through trial and error which means that success or failure appears to them to be due to sheer luck. Connections with previous problems are not recalled nor is any logic applied. Some pupils who have learning difficulties can be inflexible in their thinking and launch into a known solution which may be totally unsuitable. Again, an experienced person can first provide the plan, such as written or symbol instructions, but later can ask supportive questions, such as 'Can you remember what we did last time?' or 'Does that look as if it will work?' or 'What do you need to do next?'

Evaluating how well the solution worked can be difficult for pupils with learning difficulties, but essential if they are to learn from one problem to another. Photographs of failures and success can be a good strategy to use when teaching pupils to evaluate how well they did. Questions that are helpful range from 'What happened?' and 'How well do you think you did?' through to 'What could you put on your plan for next time?' and 'Can you think of any other way of solving the problem?'

Like the chart on the wall for 'Look, cover, think, write, check', it can be helpful for pupils to have one for problem-solving too. It is likely to be most effective if it is devised and written with the children themselves but below there is a sequence suggested by Bransford *et al.* (1986, cited in Ashman and Conway 1993):

IDEAL
I for identify (that a problem exists)
D for Define (the features of the problem)
E for Explore (how to solve the problem)
L for Look (to monitor progress)

Conclusions

The strategies that have been the focus of this chapter are needed by all learners, not just those with learning difficulties. Making the strategies transparent will be helpful for the whole class and improve everyone's learning. The skills and self-understanding that are gained from learning the strategies can be used in many different circumstances across the curriculum. They are, in fact, 'door openers' for learners. Once they are mastered and used effectively, they open doors to all learning. Some pupils will always need support to use the strategies effectively and some will find it difficult to generalise them to use in other contexts, but that does not mean that they should not be taught as much about them as possible.

Rachel has profound intellectual impairment and is at an early stage of development. She is learning about cause and effect, the bedrock of problem-solving. Her teacher has devised many activities that encourage her to develop understanding of cause and effect, such as using a switch to activate a tape recorder playing favourite music and playing turn-taking games with adults and peers. Her teacher is also consistently interpreting a low vocalisation to mean 'more' or 'I like this' which she hopes will develop into a means for Rachel to request activities and objects.

Rachel is likely to need the help and support of other people throughout her life, but if she can gain a little control over her surroundings through using computers and people, the quality of her life will be raised. She may never become a competent problem-solver but she may be able to use her grasp of cause and effect to help others to help her.

As the process of learning how to learn is so important, it is disappointing how few IEPs and targets contain reference to them. So many individual programmes relate entirely to content, such as learning a certain number of words or sounds, or mastering computation or sitting still for increasing amounts of time. Programmes for increasing memory, questioning, learning to map concepts and problem-solving would be more generalisable and more fundamental to learning itself.

Juanita has the following targets in her educational programme based on her IEP for which learning strategies were identified as a priority along with communication:

- to answer 'why?' questions both in whole-class interactive sessions and in small group work;
- to plan activities with the help of the symbol programme on the computer;
- to respond to 'what do you have to do next?' by referring to the plan.

The targets are addressed across the curriculum by all staff who come in contact with her so she gets many opportunities to learn and to practice. Everyone contributes to recording progress, including Juanita herself.

An important aspect of focusing on learning strategies is that they can be worked on many times a day, enabling progress to be as rapid as possible, and can have payoff in many areas of the curriculum, enabling the progress to be widespread.

CHAPTER 5

Teaching approaches

In this chapter the role of the teacher will be examined in terms of how teachers can enable pupils to learn most effectively. Throughout the book, so far, there have been frequent references to what we feel teachers should be doing to meet the needs of pupils who have learning difficulties and the main message is 'whatever is best for all learners is best for those with learning difficulties'. The skills that are needed are those of effective teachers, though they may be magnified, especially for those with the most complex disabilities. They would include: good powers of observation; active listening; skilled use of questioning; good motivating skills; high expectations and the ability to offer endless opportunities for developing the next step in learning.

The topics that are covered in this chapter are:

- the role of the teacher;
- open-ended learning;
- levels of learning;
- teaching thinking;
- the teacher as mediator;
- relationships between teachers and learners.

Again these are topics which apply across the curriculum as well as across the age and ability range.

The role of the teacher

Throughout the previous chapter on learning, there were many references to teaching; to how teachers can facilitate learning. Facilitation of learning is not a passive activity. It is not about putting out equipment, providing text books and computers or merely giving information for learners to do with what they will. It is a deliberate act of assessing needs and placing teaching carefully in a way in which learners can engage with it. It is entirely child-centred; not in the way that some people chose to present that concept, as indulgent and woolly but as precise and specific to that child at that moment. It is a difficult task for teachers to 'get it right' every time but that is a challenge to be taken up, not abandoned as inappropriate. If teaching is not child-centred it will undoubtedly produce many, many failures; pupils who do not and can not fit into the vision of the perfect learner and the perfect curriculum.

It has been indicated throughout this book that many learning difficulties can actually be **created** by the education system that has grown up over the years. Some pupils are deemed to have difficulties in comparison with an arbitrarily agreed 'norm'. They are seen as additional to the 'normal' system and in need of an adapted curriculum, specialist teachers and special teaching approaches. Wishing to change this state of affairs does not necessarily deny the real intellectual impairment of some learners who will always find learning more difficult than others. Teaching groups of pupils whose needs are different from each other creates a situation where difference is accepted not treated as something special. It does not call for special teaching approaches, just good teaching approaches.

Croll and Hastings (1996: 1) suggest that 'teachers matter' and that there is no evidence to support a single best approach to teaching. Teachers will always need to be flexible, although it is recognised that individuals have preferences, hopefully based on sound evidence, reflection and self-evaluation. Many texts on teaching pupils with learning difficulties have emphasised the importance of one particular approach to teaching, which is often labelled a 'behavioural approach' (Farrell 1997), at the expense of others which may be equally or more helpful. The behavioural approach is built on a view of learning which relies on tasks being broken down into its constituent parts. Thus reading is learned through mastering individual letters, groups of letters or whole words which are then built up into phrases, sentences and paragraphs.

As was seen in the previous chapter, not all people learn in this analytical manner. Some prefer to learn in a holistic way: appreciating the whole before the parts make sense. Good teachers make use of many ways of learning, offering pupils the chance to use their preferred way of learning as well as developing others. Good teachers also recognise that some approaches are better suited to specific tasks than others. For example, learning spellings, multiplication tables, chemical periodic tables and the order of historical facts are best learned through rote means so that they can be produced at will during other learning: but deciding on the meaning of historical events, understanding cause and effect in Chemistry or solving a joint problem in Technology might call upon knowledge learned though rote skills but will need analytical, evaluative and problem-solving skills over and above this knowledge.

Open-ended learning

Sometimes teaching will need learning to be defined in advance, such as in learning the names of the notes in a conventional musical scale but at others teaching will be dependent upon the learning being open-ended, such as in composing a piece of music or evaluating how well a piece evokes the sea. Certainly some of the learning to think, that was central to the previous chapter, is difficult to define in advance but that does not invalidate it as learning. Thinking is also difficult to observe at the end of the learning as it is mainly about the processes that are going on as part of the learning. Teachers can find this lack of tangible evidence unnerving, especially in the current climate of observable targets and levels of learning. However, thinking can be observed, perhaps through several examples of its use or through engaging the learners in the expression of their thinking. Just because it is difficult to measure, does not make open-ended learning an inappropriate teaching method, even with those who find learning difficult.

Mrs Kaur is working with a pupil (Jasmine) in her class, using a teaching approach called 'intensive interaction'. Jasmine is at a very early stage of development and this approach, which is based on the interaction between typically developing infants and caregivers, has been deemed appropriate for her needs. In the short sessions that Mrs Kaur and Jasmine have together, they engage in turn-taking games and activities that encourage Jasmine to anticipate what is going to happen next. So, for example, Mrs Kaur waits until she gets Jasmine's attention then she rolls her over and drums gently on her back. She rolls her back again, they laugh together and the teacher waits for her to attend to her again before she repeats the game. After a while she waits rather longer, hoping that Jasmine will show anticipation of what is going to happen by laughing, moving herself, making a sound of anything that will tell her that she is understanding what is happening.

Mrs Kaur did not know in advance what she was going to use as an activity to teach anticipation. If she had planned that she wanted three indications of anticipation out of a possible five during a specified activity, she may have been disappointed. She is working with Jasmine in a natural manner, using her mood and following her lead. Jasmine may not have reacted to the rolling and drumming on her back. That would have been fine. Mrs Kaur would have tried something else and/or watched to see if Jasmine started an activity herself.

Mrs Kaur is using an open-ended teaching approach which enables the child to dictate the learning she is ready for. She is providing the opportunity for the child to learn and is actively involved in creating the learning with her.

It may be tempting for the reader to say that open-ended learning is fine for a pupil who is so obviously at an early stage of development, but in a crowded curriculum with the pressure of improving 'standards', how can this be possible with those pupils who are, for example, struggling to learn to read?

Ms Hobbs encourages her learning readers to read books that are beyond their individual abilities to read alone. They read all together and when they meet words they don't understand Ms Hobbs demonstrates how they can read a little further to see if the word (and its meaning) becomes clear. She encourages them to work together to retell the story on tape or through pictures so that they can achieve more together than they can alone. She helps them to write through supporting them with mapping and planning. All the children are enthusiastic about reading and are making progress, although the actual reading level of each child is different.

In these lessons, Ms Hobbs does not present highly structured activities for the struggling readers, based on breaking down reading to letters and words. She engages them with interesting and stretching material with which they can achieve within a group situation. Several of them can not read the material on their own but they see themselves as readers and as contributors to group reading and writing. When she first moved from structured to open-ended teaching, Ms Hobbs found it hard. She said 'it's hard as a teacher who's trying to be that person in front of the class teaching, controlling everything, to turn loose that control' (Keefe 1996).

In the above account, taken from a book called *Label-Free Learning*, there are several aspects to Ms Hobbs's teaching which are useful to emphasise.

- She enabled achievement through encouraging group effort.
- She encouraged alternatives to writing when recording activities.
- She took a whole-language approach to reading.
- She boosted pupil self-esteem.
- She provided support for developing learning strategies.

She did **not**:

- isolate the pupils who found reading difficult;
- break down their learning into small steps;
- specifically decide what they were going to learn in advance;
- measure individuals' work against a so-called 'norm';
- expect everyone to learn on their own.

It is hard to break free from the abiding need to teach pupils with learning difficulties through a small-steps, structured approach in isolation from their peers. It feels safe to decide what is to be learned and how, and it feels as if teachers are doing something special and different that justifies being called 'special education'. It is helpful for everyone, for some of the time, to break learning into bite-sized chunks, to look in detail at a specific aspect of learning and to decide that twenty French vocabulary words will be learned with an error of 10 per cent, but this is not the only way to learn. It implies that learning only takes place when teachers are teaching and that is patently not so.

Levels of learning

Although teachers do not have to be present all the time, they **are** responsible for making sure that the level of learning is right for the learner. The five levels that follow are useful when planning learning progress (Wedell, 1995a).

1. *Initial understanding* – at this initial level of learning, the important issues is to help a pupil understand what a learning task involves, what the purpose (aim) of it is, and what a successful outcome might be. Teaching needs to be explicit, and if necessary tasks should be broken down into small, but meaningful steps.

2. *Acquisition* – teaching at the level of initial understanding is interwoven with acquisitional learning. Teaching at this level tends to emphasise the development of accuracy in learning new skills. Sometimes too, particularly with older pupils, sensitive 'unlearning' needs to take place and be replaced with a more successful approach. Teaching methods likely to be useful at this level are: demonstration and modelling, together with close prompting (which can be verbal, physical or both). This prompting is vitally important in the fostering of co-attention, where both pupil and teacher engage fully with a learning task. Pupils with learning difficulties will find such co-attentional activity very helpful at this stage.

3. *Fluency* – once acquisitional learning is taking place, teaching should aim to help a pupil to work more fluently. In other words, to refine skills to the point where they can be used accurately and almost automatically. Regular, routine short periods of practice (learning by 'doing') are likely to be helpful at this level of learning. Learning activity will not necessarily need to be closely directed all of the time, but will need to be monitored and supported.

4. *Maintenance* – though fluency in learning can be established through regular practice, skills, knowledge and understanding can easily be forgotten, or at least involve 'slippage' and become fragmentary. It is therefore important to recognise that 'overlearning', or practice over extended periods of time may be important for many pupils with learning difficulties. A careful balance needs to be achieved here. On the one hand, routine and regular practice needs to take place, but on the other, this activity should not become too boring or basic. One way of helping pupils to maintain their learning is to encourage them to undertake homework, particularly during holiday periods. This work should focus on confidence building and be both familiar to and possible for the pupil. From a psychological perspective, overlearning activity is particularly important for pupils with learning difficulties for it provides an opportunity to develop more efficient memory usage.

5. *Generalising* – once successful learning has been evidenced, particularly in targeted, or priority areas, it is important for teaching to encourage the use of skills, knowledge and understanding in new contexts, and through the use of new materials. At this level, pupils are learning to problem-solve, and to use what they know flexibly.

Teaching thinking

In the previous chapter, much time was spent on exploring the ways in which pupils can learn how to solve problems, think and learn how to learn. This chapter will include discussion on how teachers might **teach** thinking, learning and problem-solving.

It seems strange to ask whether thinking should be taught in schools. Is that not what schools are there for; to teach children to think? That may be so, yet there is not universal agreement about **how** to teach thinking and it is not often that teaching the **transferable** skills of thinking is seen as pivotal to pupils who have learning difficulties. More often **specific** skills are cited as important for pupils with learning difficulties.

Feuerstein's (1980) *Instrumental Enrichment* and Blagg *et al.*'s (1988) *Somerset Thinking Skills Course* are two examples of ways in which thinking can be taught directly and specifically with pupils with learning difficulties in mind. Each course demands the isolation of thinking skills which can then be generalised. They make considerable use of paper and pencil exercises to, for example, look for patterns in a series of dots or make deductions about the occupants of a house from their dustbin. Teachers are not convinced (and research has not confirmed), though, that these courses are helpful as it is difficult for thinking to take place in a vacuum (Burden 1998). Gardner (1983) argues that there are at least seven different forms of intelligence and that if we want to teach pupils to become effective scientific, mathematical or musical thinkers then we should teach thinking through those subjects and not in isolation.

Reading Recovery is a well-documented example of teaching thinking and problem-solving strategies to pupils who are the least able readers at the age of six. Reading Recovery is **not** a programme that depends upon isolating letters, words and parts of words. Teachers learn to look carefully at how children are reading, the strengths they have and the miscues they make. They are then asked to support the thinking and learning of the children with the aim of creating independent learners. So they are asked to:

- stay with what the child already knows until she or he is fluent (resist introducing new learning);
- set new tasks that are a little more difficult but that allow existing knowledge to be used;
- provide a bridge between the child's existing knowledge and the demands of the new task (give help in organising attention and activity);
- give instruction based on enabling the child to problem-solve (e.g. hints relating to child's current knowledge; focusing attention on the salient features);
- reduce help and encourage self-correction (use questions that **assist** the child rather than **assess**; allow risk-taking);
- encourage generalisation (helping the child to draw analogies with previous experiences and related problems) (from Birtwhistle 1998).

Survey results of the outcomes of Reading Recovery (Lyons *et al.* 1993) found that the most successful teachers:

- allowed more time for independent problem-solving and knew when to be quiet;
- are more persistent in questioning (in a way to make pupils think) and in prompting pupils;
- ask children to self-check and evaluate outcomes.

Teachers who had fewer successful children were found to focus on letters, words and sentences rather than on strategies. They encouraged dependence on help from the adult and on remembering rather than on problem-solving.

The pupil strategies that were encouraged by the successful teachers were those that are used by experienced readers:

- inferencing (making predictions using prior knowledge combined with information available from the text);
- identifying important information (finding the critical facts and details in different types of texts);
- monitoring (being aware that there is a problem and employing a strategy, e.g. re-reading a paragraph that does not make sense);
- summarising (pulling together information from a long passage);
- question-generating (asking themselves questions to be able to synthesise the text).

Birtwhistle (1998) suggests that these strategies should be regarded as helpful in constructing meaning in all curriculum areas.

The teacher as mediator

Teaching children to think, to learn and to problem-solve involves teachers in the role of 'mediator', that is someone who helps learners to move into the next level of understanding. Vygotsky suggested that teaching was most effective in what he called 'the zone of proximal development' (Wood 1998). He measured this zone by finding out what a child can do independently and what she or he can do with help. The zone of proximal development is that area between the two. If teaching is placed there, it will be close enough to current thinking for the child to be able to build on it, but far enough away to be challenging. Teachers can provide support (or scaffolding) for children to be able to succeed and this can be gradually withdrawn until success is achieved independently. In this way, teachers mediate between children and their tasks, asking questions and encouraging thought and problem-solving.

Teachers who see themselves as mediators of learning help pupils to:

- see the significance and value of learning activities to themselves;
- see the learning intentions of activities;
- approach activities in a focused and self-directed way;

- feel competent in their abilities to cope with learning tasks;
- control and regulate their own learning using self-directed and appropriate skills and strategies;
- cooperate with each other;
- recognise their own individuality;
- foster a sense of belonging to a community.   (Williams and Burden 1998).

They do not see themselves as the holders of the keys to knowledge and controllers of learning in the classroom. They believe that learners construct their own understanding of the world and that teachers help them to do that.

Mediators share learning with pupils. They demonstrate the use of transferable skills, for example through using questioning to direct an enquiry or through recalling previous activities that might help in a current task. They provide opportunities for learning to take place, for example through deliberately sabotaging a known routine to provoke problem-solving or organising a debate on a controversial topic. They provide support for pupils to succeed, for example through asking questions such as 'what should you do next?' or 'what happened last time?' or through suggesting an alternative line of enquiry.

Mr Haig works with a History class. He fills a suitcase with personal items from a previous era and invites the children to become detectives and identify the owner of the suitcase. As they go through the items he asks questions such as 'Does that remind you of something we looked at last week?' and 'Who might use something like that?' He also invites them to ask questions of him and of each other, giving them positive feedback when the questions are particularly effective.

He helps the class to accumulate the evidence by asking them to record it in a simple table on the flipchart. They use a mixture of words and sketches so that everyone can read it. Part-way through the lesson, Mr Haig divides the class into mixed ability groups and invites them to investigate a few items in more detail. They use sources that they have been introduced to in earlier lessons. Each group shares their information (using a mixture of written words, sketches and spoken words) and gradually the mystery unfolds. Finally Mr Haig introduces one more item that he has deliberately withheld, telling the class that he wanted to see if they could use their powers of detection without it. At the end of the lesson, Mr Haig helps the pupils to evaluate how well they succeeded and how well they worked together. They discuss the most useful questions and the most useful sources for information.

Relationships between teachers and learners

When teachers are working as mediators, they are learning as well as teaching. They need to watch children's learning very carefully as they build a picture of the support that is needed for them to move on. Teachers need to be responsive, coaxing and pushing in turn, leaving pupils with questions to answer but not allowing them to experience failure alone. Much can be learned from mistakes, but not unless you have someone near you to help you to learn.

Teachers also need to be explicit in what they say to pupils. Watson's (1996) research on pupil reflection (focused on pupils with learning difficulties) showed that pupils showed greater frustration when teachers used vague language and were not able to tune into pupil thinking. Sharing the same focus of attention seemed to be important to the quality of the exchange and of the pupils' thinking. Watson clearly says that pupils need to know what they are doing and why. There will be poor thinking if all that matters is to get the task done. Watson also suggests that the teachers who encourage the best thinking in their classroom use talk that is:

- responsive and explicit;
- tuned into what pupils say;
- asking pupils for explanations and justifications;
- pointing out analogies, consistencies and inconsistencies;
- raising metacognitive awareness (thinking about their own thinking).

Helping pupils to feel good about themselves and their learning is also very important. It is easy for pupils to feel inadequate if they are not coping with classroom activities. They are reluctant to ask for help and admit their difficulties. Teachers who encourage admissions of difficulty from everyone (including themselves) and present plenty of activities to which there is no one right answer are often the most successful. Group work and the expectations that groups of people will be more successful than individuals is also likely to be successful. Encouraging support from peers helps to create a general ethos of positive expectations as will opportunities for deliberate celebration of pupils' strengths, individuality and differences. Praise for good thinking, especially in face of a hard task, can boost self-esteem and make further effort more likely.

Conclusions

This chapter on teaching has not contained special methods for teaching pupils with learning difficulties. The pace of learning may have to be slower, the amount learned may be less, the starting point may be different but good teaching is vital whoever the learner might be. All pupils need teachers who can select, from the vast array of approaches, the best tool for the task. The emphasis in this chapter has been on teaching transferable skills such as thinking, learning and problem-solving, but that does not mean that it is never important to teach specific skills. However, specific skills are not usually easily generalisable for pupils who have learning difficulties and are best embedded in the contexts within which they will be used. Consider, though the story of Ben reported by Bayliss (1998).

Ben, who has severe learning difficulties, was taught cooking skills through task analysis at his special school but could not generalise them sufficiently to cook sausages and chips at the college of further education. His teachers tried simple scaffolding and supported Ben with prompts and suggestions. This was no more successful than the first approach as he still burned the sausages when they removed the support. Then his teachers tried simple sketch recipe cards which provided him with constant support that he could use at his own pace and cut out any complicated and potentially confusing spoken language. Alongside these they taught him the transferable skills of selective attention, responding to and using questions and planning. His teachers also improved in their support, changing from using questions like 'Are the sausages turning black?' – which was designed to prevent them from burning but actually encouraged Ben to wait until they were – to 'What do you have to do next?' when he needed to turn the sausages, thus helping him to succeed.

Teaching pupils to think can give them a lifelong set of skills and strategies which they can use in countless situations. Some people with learning difficulties may never be able to live and work as self-sufficiently as the majority of the population but with the right kind of support geared to their needs they will be able to take some control over their own lives.

CHAPTER 6

Organisation for learning

In this chapter it is intended to explore the organisational needs of pupils with learning difficulties (across the ability range) in mainstream classes. It is helpful to put together what has been said about learning and about teaching with the third side to the triangle, the environment. It is very clear that mainstream school environments do need to be changed if **all** pupils are to be able to learn in them. This change applies to people as well as to buildings and furniture.

The topics that will be covered in this chapter are:

- the physical environment;
- pupil groupings (including timetabling and moving about the school);
- learning support assistants;
- working with other people (including families).

Physical environment

If pupils with learning difficulties are going to be meaningfully included in mainstream schools, attention will need to be paid to designing and maintaining the physical environment. It is not just a matter of building ramps for wheelchair-users, wide doorways and facilities for changing pupils who are incontinent, although these are, of course, important. It is essential that the environment is designed to aid those with difficulties in learning: to help them move around the school, use cues for daily life and for supporting their learning.

Surinder is eleven years old and has severe learning difficulties. He uses a rollator (walking frame) to walk and wears boots with callipers. He is continent if enabled to visit the toilet frequently. He has a reading vocabulary of 25 symbols and writes using a symbol program on the computer. He has a good understanding of everyday spoken language, especially if signs are used to support conversations. He responds best if the speaker makes sure that he is attending to what is being said. His spoken language is telegraphic and accompanied by occasional signs and gestures but he gets his meaning across most of the time. Surinder's vision is partially corrected with glasses but he requires large printed symbols for reading and an ordered environment to move around independently.

From this brief pen picture, it is clear that Surinder needs an environment which is enhanced in certain ways. It was deliberately written in a positive way so that the support that he needs is apparent. It would be easy to describe him as having cerebral palsy, visual impairment, limited language and not able to read and write, but that would not be helpful when designing his learning environment. To be able to function and to learn, Surinder needs the following:

- a rollator with space around the classroom and school for him to be able to manoeuvre it;
- regular physiotherapy (not necessarily always from a physiotherapist) to maintain and improve his mobility;
- a toilet that is close to the classroom and regular reminders to use it; this would need a grab rail and plenty of space for the rollator;
- books that have large symbols as well as words and have an interest level of an eleven year old but text for a beginner reader;
- use of a personal computer, a concept keyboard and a symbol writing program which produces large symbols;
- people around him to use signs when they talk to him and to speak directly to him – he may not attend to general instructions to the class;
- people around him to be patient and wait for him to get his meaning across;
- time to respond to directions (both thinking time and also time physically to get from one place to another);
- regular speech and language therapy (not necessarily always from a speech and language therapist) to maintain and improve his speech and language;
- furniture to be of contrasting colours to each other and to the background;
- at least some of the wall displays to be clear and uncluttered.

Surinder may need a lot of support to be able to function and learn in a mainstream school but he has many other needs which are exactly the same as every child. He needs to feel that he is physically comfortable and personally safe; that he is a valued member of the school and his views are important; he needs interesting topics to study that build on his previous understanding and skills and he needs to exercise his 'growing-up muscles' like other children do as they approach adolescence and adult life. All these (and others) are important and determine the kind of learning environment that should be provided by schools and teachers.

Pupils who have a variety of learning difficulties will need all kinds of specialist support, but this support is not so specialist that it cannot be provided in schools that have been designated mainstream. Not all pupils with learning difficulties will need all of the support suggested below but the list contains a breadth of ideas.

- Use visual instructions to accompany speech. This could range from a cue word or words on card to a sign or a symbol.
- Use sentences that are clear and where the most important information comes at

the beginning, for example, 'Sssh, quietly, put your books away', for which the cue is 'sssh' with a finger on the lips and the most important word is 'quietly', followed by the instruction. It might be helpful to start with an individual name. So the instruction might run: 'Listen everyone. Lucy listen . . .'

- Use the classroom displays to provide support for writing, numbers, words for spelling, symbol timetables, clearly marked storage. Train everyone to use these supports and each other before resorting to asking an adult for help.
- Provide a distraction-free area for pupils who find it difficult to concentrate for any length of time. Just include the material that supports that session.
- Designate space for resources such as computers, wheelchairs, large books, tape recorders, physiotherapy equipment. This space needs to be easily accessible or the equipment will not be used regularly.
- Make sure there is easy access to computers and tape recorders as these may be a major support for reading and writing.
- Create trails around the school for pupils with learning difficulties and sensory impairments. Many pupils can be taught to recognise different surfaces, sound and visual clues, symbols and pictures. So for example, the trail to the cookery room could be painted on the wall (which could be a series of raised shapes) with a cue card of the symbol for cooking just outside the correct door. There could be smaller symbols (which could be raised) on the trail to remind the pupils where they are going.
- Provide the optimum seating arrangements for pupils with learning difficulties. They may be best close to the teacher but they may be best against the light so the teacher and the rest of the class are easy to see. Next to the toilet may be good for one pupil or next to a peer prepared to help or a hard-nosed peer who makes the pupil with learning difficulties fend for him or herself. It depends on the need of the individual pupil.

All these suggestions are aimed at reducing the learning difficulty and providing the right amount of support for pupils to be able to join in. They are largely preventative. For example, if a pupil is known not to respond unless she is addressed directly then build this into her support rather than constantly telling her off for not listening. It is hoped that eventually she will need this support less and less but she may need it for the whole of her school life.

Pupil groupings

This section will begin with designing individual timetables for pupils with learning difficulties and how this affects 'where' they are being taught and 'with whom'. Pupils who have mild to moderate learning difficulties may need few adaptations to the 'where' and 'with whom' aspects of their timetable as often their needs can be met through varying the pace and difficulty of the material being used with the rest of the class. They may also need human or technological support to enable them to record their ideas and some of the preventative strategies suggested in the previous section. In addition, there may be times when a small group of pupils can work in a distraction-free space, providing this does not become the norm for less able pupils. This withdrawn group may or may not consist wholly of pupils with learning difficulties. It may be a mixed group or a group of very able pupils. Varying the groupings prevents unnecessary segregation and the low expectations that often accompany the so-called 'bottom group' (Dean 1992).

Pupils with more severe learning difficulties or multiple disabilities may need much more individual consideration so that they gain the most from a mainstream education. Some of these pupils may only spend part of their day or week actually with their mainstream peers and this could be in a special school or a mainstream school. They could also be placed in a specialist unit attached to a mainstream school (or, as in Oxfordshire, a special school which is located inside a mainstream school) or in a resourced specialist class (as in Stockport), where staff experienced in meeting the needs of pupils with severe and profound learning difficulties will be working with them and advising others on how best to teach them.

Jack has profound and multiple learning difficulties and is a wheelchair-user. He communicates through smiles and other facial expressions and understands inflexion in the voice of a speaker, and a few simple labelling words such as drink, dinner and the names of his peers. He is quick to pick up on atmosphere and can join in exciting, calm and happy moments appropriately. He will respond to but not initiate interaction with others. Jack can use his hands to manipulate large equipment, though his movements are jerky and gross. He can hear sounds that are clear and relatively high-pitched. He has a concentration span of approximately two minutes when he is interested in the stimulus but needs frequent changes of activity. He shows boredom or frustration through banging his hands loudly on the table or his wheelchair. Jack is placed in a specialist class in a mainstream secondary school and is included with his more able peers for part of his week.

Again, mainly the positive aspects of Jack's learning have been emphasised as this is most helpful in determining his needs, in terms of 'where' to learn and 'with whom'.

As Jack clearly enjoys being with his peers (he has learned some of their names) it is important that he has some time when he can interact with them at a level that is appropriate for him. He needs activities that are frequently changing and that engage him at his level of development (around the 9–12 month level in a typically developing child). He is also good at reacting to atmosphere which indicates that stories, drama and music might be good aspects for working with his more able peers. Art, craft and technology, including food technology, might also be fruitful subjects for working together, anything where there is plenty of activity.

It would be good for Jack to have a mixture of locations for his learning, both specialist and mainstream. If there is a specialist resourced room, it can provide him with controlled sound and clutter which can be related directly to his level of hearing and intellectual understanding. More able peers could come to this space to work. That might be particularly appropriate when working on composing a piece of music or scene for a drama or whenever small groups of pupils are sent off to undertake a task which they take back to the whole class.

The hurly-burly of the mainstream classroom or hall would also be appropriate for Jack's learning needs for some of the time. He likes plenty going on and gets bored easily, so a busy art or design and technology session would be very stimulating. Jack could be enabled to join in group activities, despite his jerky hand movements. Cooperative groupwork (see below) would be particularly appropriate, especially 'jigsawing' where each person contributes a different part of the task so that the whole is complete when all the parts are finished (Rose 1991).

Jack is working in the art room with three other young people. (The rest of the class are also working in small groups.) Together they are making an underwater scene using a variety of media (they have to use at least three). Jack has been asked to paint the backcloth and has been given the choice of two different colours (blue and green). He is painting using both colours, sometimes one and sometimes the other. He uses a large brush and he is supported by a learning support assistant who helps him to choose colours, reach the paint and the extremes of the large piece of paper. The other three young people are cutting out material fish; creating 3D amphibians out of wire and papier mâché and a shipwreck out of polystyrene. Later Jack paints the shipwreck alongside one of the other young people. As they work, the whole group chat. Jack 'chats' with his face, watching what is going on and reacting with smiles when addressed. He giggles when one young person livens up the proceedings by pretending to dive bomb the fish with her half-made frog.

Jack cannot create an underwater scene on his own. In fact he probably has no conception of what it entails. He probably has little more idea when the picture is completed, but he has been part of a valuable learning experience. He has been able to interact with others at his own level, accomplish a task within his ability as well as having the opportunity to copy more able peers as they work at their own level.

Jack would also benefit from other kinds of groupings, although his level of learning difficulty would make it difficult for him to gain much from whole-class lessons that were not directed specifically at him. A learning support assistant (LSA) can help to individualise whole-class lessons by having tangible resources available and talking directly to Jack, pointing things out to him and interpreting his reactions. Pupils with mild or moderate learning difficulties may need elements of this kind of support but it may not need an extra adult to achieve the same effect. The teacher could make sure that interactive exchanges in whole-class lessons are graded in difficulty so that everyone in the class can be involved at least some of the time.

There are other groupings which can enable pupils with learning difficulties to be included with their more able peers.

Emma has moderate learning difficulties and is full-time in a mainstream class. She is nine years old and has a reading age of six. She writes under the teacher's writing or from a word book and can spell a few simple words without help. Emma is easily discouraged but will attempt work which is well within her capabilities. She likes topics about animals and is verbally competent in lessons where they feature. She sits next to a more able pupil (her 'buddy') who often prompts her to find words or gives her clues. This pupil will sometimes read instructions to Emma and help her read back her own writing. Sometimes they will work together in a partnership, where Emma will write a short piece to accompany her buddy's longer piece. Much work has been carried out in the class on individual differences and there is a buddy system worked out between the class members. Emma is of average ability in PE and she is a buddy for Victoria who has more severe learning difficulties and joins the group from the specialist class for that lesson.

Some teachers and parents are concerned that if more able pupils are asked to tutor less able pupils that they will be held back. There is actually no evidence to suggest that this is so. Where pupils of different abilities are paired, both can gain from the relationship (Fitz-Gibbon 1988). Explaining or demonstrating something to someone else can help that person to articulate and thus consolidate the learning. However, if the relationship is always one of tutor and taught it can breed dependency and it is advisable to vary the way in which the pairs work together as well as varying the partnerships (Galton and Williamson 1992).

Learning support assistants

Learning support assistants have already been mentioned as one of the factors in successful inclusion of pupils with learning difficulties in mainstream schools, and they are the subject of this next section.

People who support pupils in classrooms are given different names in different areas (classroom assistant, non-teaching assistant, special support assistant, educational assistant). In this book, it was decided to use the term learning support assistant (LSA) as this is currently being used by DfEE (1998). LSAs are usually hourly paid and work only the hours pupils are in the classroom; many are untrained but yet have considerable day-to-day responsibility for the education of the pupils they support. There is a fine line to be drawn between exploiting this group of staff and properly involving them in the pupils' learning. It is not right to expect them to plan (especially as the lesson is in progress), produce resources, evaluate and record progress for the pupils they work with. Neither is it right for teachers to do all this for them without consulting, expecting them to carry out their plans without question. There needs to be a balance between the two. Teachers are responsible for the learning of all the pupils in their classes but this can be shared with LSAs, who may have talents and skills which are very useful to bring to the situation (Fox 1998). There will be more on how to achieve this in the final section of this chapter where some strategies for helping teamwork to work will be discussed.

LSAs are employed in a variety of different ways. Some are designated as individual support for named pupils, others are employed for general support in the classroom. Some work part-time with more than one named child and others sometimes work with individuals and sometimes with small groups. However their time is used, it is important to consider how to give the **least** possible support to pupils with learning difficulties. 'More is not necessarily better.' If LSAs never leave the child's side, it will be difficult for that child to form relationships with peers, learn strategies for managing his or her own life or try out some of activities of which adults might not approve, but which are so important to growing up (Lorenz 1998b).

The following two scenarios (one in a primary school and the other in a secondary school) demonstrate some of the positive ways in which LSAs can enable the learning of pupils with learning difficulties.

Sean has moderate learning difficulties and is placed in a mainstream primary school. There are two other pupils in his class who need the support of an LSA and Mrs Jones is employed to work specifically with these children. Mrs Jones begins her day 15 minutes before the pupils and finishes 15 minutes after they have gone. She does not work during the lunch break and often returns home, which is very close to the school, during that hour. The half an hour a day without the children is spent with the teacher, planning, gathering resources and reporting back. Although Mrs Jones concentrates on the three pupils with learning difficulties, she often reports on the learning of other pupils.

Sean needs support for reading and writing. He needs individual instruction for part of the day as well as general support in terms of resources (simplified texts and access to the computer for writing). Mrs Jones and the teacher share these between them, so that sometimes Sean is taught by the teacher and sometimes by the LSA. Sean also experiences small group work with the other pupils with learning difficulties as well as working with his more able peers. Wherever he is working, Mrs Jones will be watching to make sure that he is gaining the most from the learning situation. She constantly judges how much support he needs and is sensitive about withdrawing when he does not need her. She will discuss his changing needs with the teacher in the planning sessions.

Nadia has severe learning difficulties and is placed in the resourced class of a mainstream secondary school. She spends approximately a third of her week with her mainstream peers, although they are actually a year younger than her.

This is an Art lesson which four pupils with SLD attend with an LSA. Nadia sits at a table with her friends, one from the SLD class and two from the mainstream class. The LSA sits at this table but supports anyone who needs help. The lesson begins with reminders of the previous lesson. Nadia puts up her hand to answer which she manages with a little prompting from the LSA.

The teacher makes sure everyone has a chance to answer, slows the pace when asking Nadia or the other from the SLD class and accepts less developed answers from them than from the rest of the class. Sometimes she directly asks pupils and sometimes she asks everyone and picks someone to answer. Nadia is obviously familiar with this technique and reacts appropriately. After a few minutes, Nadia put her head down on her arms as if she is tired with the demands of the lesson. The LSA leans over to her and talks gently in her ear. In a minute or two, Nadia lifts her head and is ready to join in again.

When the discussion session is over, everyone settles down to their artwork. Nadia needs very little support from the LSA as she is used to working in the artroom and knows where the equipment is kept. The teacher moves around the class helping individuals and asking questions which prompt the pupils to evaluate their efforts. The LSA also asks questions and makes suggestions and she encourages interactions between the pupils with SLD and the mainstream pupils.

When Nadia returns to her resourced class, the LSA supports her as she tells the teacher what has occurred and helps her to remember what she learned. Together they fill in her record sheet which is then shared briefly with the teacher.

From these scenarios (and other experience), it is possible to set out some suggestions for working effectively with LSAs.

• Clarify the role of the LSA and the teacher so that both are clear about what they are doing in the classroom. Is the assistant supporting the teacher, a group of pupils, an individual or the whole class? And if it is all of these, when?
• Set aside time for the teacher and LSA to plan and record together, even though the bulk of the paperwork will be the responsibility of the teacher. It is certainly not effective (nor fair) to expect LSAs to come to a lesson unprepared and just adapt things as they go along. They need to be consulted and good use should be made of their experience.
• If an LSA works with a designated pupil, it will not be beneficial for the pupil to be 'velcroed' to the LSA. Even for a pupil with profound and multiple learning difficulties who needs a mediator to be involved in all activities, it should be possible to encourage direct interaction with able-bodied peers, especially if time has been spent on helping the mainstream pupils tune into the idiosyncratic communication used by the child with PMLD.
• In some circumstances it may be better for LSAs to be attached to departments, especially in secondary schools. In that way they can become skilled in one particular subject and can offer more targeted support. It could also help to encourage teenagers with learning difficulties to be less dependent on one person as they will meet several as they go from subject to subject.

LSAs are not cheap teachers, they can offer very valuable support to the learning process in the classroom. They build up experience and can be very skilled in 'leading from behind' – stepping in to help only when it is really necessary. Teachers should never lose sight of the responsibility they have for all the pupils in their class, as seems to have happened in this next example.

Consider this scenario (NB this is **not** good practice):

There are three pupils with learning difficulties in this mainstream primary classroom. They work at a table in the centre of the classroom with an LSA. The teacher teaches the rest of the class but leaves the LSA to teach the group of pupils with learning difficulties. The teacher hardly ever speaks to the pupils with learning difficulties but she does sometimes discuss their work with the LSA.

This teacher appears to have abdicated her responsibility and has left the LSA almost completely unsupported.

If LSAs are not cheap teachers, neither are they general 'dogsbodies', mixing paint, wiping tears and tidying the library. They have an important role to play in providing the environment that is supportive of learning. They can be an amanuensis (write for someone), make specialist resources, remind pupils to listen, share tasks to ensure satisfaction through completion, present the world to pupils in an accessible way (through touch, through signs) and provide individual instruction just at the right moment.

Working with other people

This chapter is concluded with a section on working with other people in the school. These people can range from therapists and psychologists to peripatetic specialists and families. Pupils with learning difficulties often have many people involved in their care and education. The more support needs they have the greater the number of people involved.

Sasha is thirteen and has complex needs. She has moderate learning difficulties that are compounded by hearing impairment and language delay. All the following people are connected with her care and education:

- family
- form tutor
- subject teachers
- SENCO
- heads of department
- LSAs
- specialist teacher for hearing impairment
- educational audiologist
- consultant audiologist

- speech and language therapist
- paediatrician
- family doctor.

With so many people involved, it is very difficult to keep communication going between them. Sasha's parents have opted to become coordinators of her care and education and encourage everyone to keep them informed about whatever happens. They keep a record of all the decision-making visits made by or to anyone on the list, giving copies to the school at regular intervals. Sasha's form tutor has undertaken to coordinate what happens at school and regularly relays information home. As everyone is working in a coordinated manner, Sasha has an integrated approach to her care and education. For example, the LSA who works with Sasha in the English department, carries out daily speech and language work planned with the speech and language therapist. The LSA keeps brief records of progress which she gives to the form tutor.

Not all parents of pupils with learning difficulties can become coordinators of their child's care and education. Some just do not have the time, others are overwhelmed by the difficulties faced by their offspring, yet others have learning difficulties of their own. For some parents, especially those facing poverty, unemployment and social deprivation, it is a challenge to relate to schools and teachers at all; others are tireless in their search for a 'cure' for their child or outspoken in their demands for a certain placement or teaching approach. Whatever their circumstances, all parents need to be kept informed about the progress of their child and every family has information about their child that would be useful for others to know (Hornby 1995). Communication between families and school is vital, however much the families can be actively involved. Schools need to cultivate an atmosphere of non-judgment of families, while keeping communication channels open and encouraging as much decision-making as possible.

While families can be involved at different levels with their child's education and care, this is not an option for professionals. Even if they see the child infrequently, they have a duty to work as closely as they can with those who are in daily contact (Lacey and Lomas 1993).

In the above example about Sasha, the peripatetic teacher of the hearing impaired visits the school every half term. While she is in the school, she works for an hour with Sasha, the LSA from the English department and the form tutor. Together they review her needs and plan the next half term's work. The visiting teacher is responsible for writing up the notes and she sends them to the form tutor and informs the staff who work with Sasha and Sasha's parents. Next time Sasha's parents go with her to the consultant they briefly summarise progress made at school. Following that visit, they bring the school up to date with decisions made.

Once a year, there is a multidisciplinary meeting where the following people meet to review Sasha's Individual Education Plan (IEP):

- family
- form tutor
- SENCO
- LSA from the English department
- specialist teacher for hearing impairment
- speech and language therapist.

Together they plan for the following year and, after hearing Sasha's opinion, the paperwork is completed by the form tutor and the SENCO. Decisions are forwarded to all the other staff who teach Sasha.

There are some strategies to help the team who are trying to work together (school and families; teacher and LSA; SENCO and visiting teachers):

- People who work together need time to talk. This might, for example, have to be taken away from time spent with the child, but it may be a much better use of the time, so that the subsequent teaching time is more profitably used.
- Time needs to be considered as flexible. Visiting professionals do not have to work directly with the child for a short time once a week. They could work with the child and his or her classroom staff for a longer time less frequently. During this time they can observe what is happening now, make suggestions, pass on skills and ensure that the child is receiving the best service all the time (not just when the specialist is available).
- When people work together they adopt a problem-solving approach where they each contribute to understanding the problem and conceiving of a solution.
- Everyone working with an individual pupil is fully aware of each others' roles, their constraints and ways of working. This can be time-consuming when people first begin to work together but it is likely to deflect potential difficulties in working together in the future.
- No-one can work effectively together with other people in schools without active management support. Managers need to be prepared to allow for investment of time for pay off later; provide cover for meetings; write clear job descriptions; give easy access to telephones; have flexible notions of working with families; provide training in teamwork (Lacey 1998).

Conclusions

This chapter has covered many aspects of working effectively with pupils who have learning difficulties. Including them in mainstream schools does mean that practice, in many places, will have to change but everything that has been written about in this chapter happens somewhere in this country. Schools are adapting their physical and learning environment, and staff are beginning to develop innovative ways of working together to meet the needs of pupils who may face several difficulties in learning.

Some of the children already placed in mainstream schools are learning to adapt to life as they find it there, but so-called 'normalisation' is not just about one-way traffic. Schools hold the keys to opening their doors to pupils with learning difficulties. They will also have to change, as will their perceptions of who can and cannot benefit from an inclusive education.

CHAPTER 7

Communications

The setting up of clear channels of communication for both staff and pupils is a major theme of this book. One crucial area, the importance of information and communication technology for pupils with learning difficulties, has not, however, been touched upon.

Information and communication technology

As information and communication technology becomes more sophisticated and government funds are made available to schools for the purchase of computers, the awareness of its significance in helping to meet the communication needs of pupils with learning difficulties in mainstream schools is increasing. ICT not only provides alternative methods of compensating for the lack of ability to communicate, but can also be used to support curriculum access in a number of exciting and innovative ways.

The use of computers can be incorporated **directly** into teaching, as the range of software available can support differentiated levels of learning. Traditionally, most software could only be accessed through the use of a keyboard or a mouse, but easily accessible software for those pupils with poor motor skills is now available. Peripherals, including switches, rollerballs, joysticks, concept keyboards, touch screens and infra-red devices (usually worn on the head), are available for accessing computers. These in addition to the resources now available to support pupils who may have physical or severe intellectual difficulties. Integrated learning systems are being developed for those who can spend 'time on task' with minimal assistance. Such 'integrated' packages include computer-based curriculum content, record-keeping systems and the management of software. The idea of giving pupils with learning difficulties autonomous programmes has obvious attractions, but Lewis (1999) warns that such an approach should be treated with caution as it could encourage the teacher 'to abdicate responsibility for pupil's learning' (p. 153).

Virtual reality enables pupils to access simulated learning environments and has been developed for the rehabilitation of pupils with physical disabilities in order to access physical-therapy and wheelchair training. (For a practical account of the use of computers and technology for pupils with limited physical movement see Pickles (1998) *Managing the Curriculum for Children with Severe Motor Difficulties*.) The Internet, email and the World Wide Web (e.g. the National Grid for Learning) all help pupils with learning difficulties to access curriculum materials and, in the case of email, develop social and communication skills in innovative ways.

ICT can also be used **indirectly** to support pupils with learning difficulties. Staff now have the opportunity to access computer software which can provide information on specific teaching and assessment approaches, in addition to guidance on the design and administration of individually focused learning programmes. Web-based resources also provide invaluable up-to-date information on specific aspects of special needs education; for example, *Contact a Family* (a family support network) is an Internet-based resource service with information on specific disabilities and rare conditions. Although the information is designed primarily for family users, it is also valuable for educational professionals, and contains links to yet more information, and 'contact and self-help groups'. Its address is: http://www.cafamily.org.uk/dirworks.html

Another indirect source of information is provided by Internet-based email-interest and discussion groups. The SENCO Forum, for example, although designed to bring SENCOs together, does not focus exclusively on their needs, provides a helpful source of information for a range of professionals (and parents), and has the added advantage of putting staff, who work in similar circumstances, in touch with each other. The Internet address of the forum (http://mailbase.ac.uk/lists/senco-forum/) provides information on joining various issue-based discussion groups.

Some Internet-based information needs to be approached cautiously, as it often has a specific perspective. Nevertheless, it is open to public scrutiny, and its quality is constantly improving. The time is approaching when all teachers of pupils with learning difficulties should be able to access Internet sources of information in their schools on a routine basis, as easily as other educational resources. Centres offering help and advice to teachers of pupils within the whole continuum of special educational needs are given in the Appendix, Useful addresses.

Communications between staff

The teaching of pupils with learning difficulties in mainstream schools is a whole-school issue and requires total commitment. Every member of staff must play a part by not only taking responsibility for **every** pupil, but by participating in the process of communication. The individual class teacher should, therefore, be part of a team which provides peer support within the school. Creese *et al.* (1997), from their research indicating that such teams prevent the isolation of individual teachers and, at the same time, aid professional development through enhanced discussion and collaborative planning, have encouraged the setting up of teacher support teams for SEN in both primary and secondary schools. Such teams help to ensure that knowledge, gained from everyday experiences in the teaching and learning of pupils with learning difficulties, can be shared. Beveridge (1999) also stresses the importance of setting up systematic procedures in order to ensure that staff work from 'shared information with a common sense of purpose' (p. 56).

When setting up discussion groups and team meetings, it is important to spend time on preliminaries, such as understanding the different points of views of the members, agreeing on the modes of communication between them, common aims for the group and the purpose of individual meetings. Many support groups or 'after school meetings' have failed to thrive because members are unclear about their purpose; they feel that attending the meetings make unreasonable demands on them or that the sessions just do not meet their support needs. Successful support groups and team meetings have a clear agenda that reflects the needs of the members, are run by an effective chairperson, enable decisions to be made (where appropriate) and have an atmosphere of trust so that members can feel safe about sharing their difficulties. Well-run support groups can be very effective in enabling communication about the learning needs of pupils, especially the needs of those who find learning difficult.

One of the best uses of such a group is in joint problem-solving. Sometimes the needs of pupils are too complex for one person to solve alone but shared understanding and information can often help to point to the way forward. It is said that 'the whole is better than the sum of the parts' and this can be so in successful joint problem-solving. Teachers do not have to struggle with the challenge of teaching pupils with learning difficulties on their own, they can and should tap the enormous wealth of understanding, knowledge and experience of those around them.

Learning from each other can be a vital aspect of support groups and classroom teams. Not only can this learning be achieved through meetings but also through working alongside each other. Most newly qualified teachers have opportunities to observe more experienced colleagues at work and it is important that this includes their work with pupils with learning difficulties. However, observation is not just important during induction but should continue to be built into professional development throughout teachers' careers. Pairing staff for mutual observation can be very effective as can team teaching with an element of observation built in. As an alternative, or in addition, lessons can be videotaped and discussed in a supportive atmosphere. This can certainly be useful for identifying pupil needs and enables repeated showing of the clips with colleagues who may be able to help with ways forward.

Some of the colleagues who may be able to help in joint problem-solving may be employed by agencies outside the school. It is important to build up a network of contacts with whom teachers can consult either formally or informally. Sometimes a phone call to an advisory teacher or an educational psychologist can open up a new avenue of thinking which could then avoid the need for a formal case conference. Again, sharing video clips with staff outside the school may enable them to contribute without having to find an afternoon to visit. An email discussion such as those on the SENCO Forum might also be a quick way to enlist the help of others. The most important message is that asking for help and support is not only sensible but necessary if pupils' learning needs are to be met and that there are several different ways in which this support can be provided.

The *Code of Practice* (DfE 1994) provided the basis for systematic support-procedures, and the requirement for the identification of a SENCO in each mainstream school ensures that the work of individual class-teachers is encouraged. Important questions about the school's policies for the identification and provision for pupils with SEN, are raised in the Foreword to this book, and the responsibilities of the SENCO in direct relation to the Code can be summed up as:

- the day-to-day operation of monitoring and assessment procedures;
- liaison with, and advice to, colleagues;
- the maintenance of the SEN register, and the monitoring of SEN records;
- liaison with parents of children with SEN;
- contributing to the professional development of colleagues;
- liaison with external agencies.

Features of good practice (based on DfEE 1997) should include such procedures as collaborating with colleagues on specific problems; being proactive in offering support; teaching and co-teaching supporting regular 'out of class times' for discussion; providing procedural information and help with resources.

The responsibilities of the class teacher in the Code dovetails into those of the SENCO and includes:

- recording concerns;
- gathering information;
- taking account of the views of parents and pupils;
- adapting teaching approaches;
- increased differentiation;
- working with external agencies.

The list may look a little daunting but, as already stated, the work of the class teacher and the SENCO are complementary and these procedures are part of a collaborative approach. Important as they are they do not guarantee that pupils with learning difficulties are valued and respected, and only go some way towards ensuring that their teaching and learning experiences are effective.

Conclusions

This book has contained several messages for teachers who are inexperienced in teaching pupils with learning difficulties in mainstream schools. Perhaps the most important is that pupils of all abilities can be educated together. They may not share the same classroom and the same lessons all day, every day, but for most pupils it is unnecessary to receive their education in a segregated setting.

Teaching pupils with a wide range of abilities and needs can be very demanding of their teachers, but we have ventured to suggest that, in essence, teaching those with learning difficulties is not so much special as **deliberate**. Most of the approaches to teaching we have advocated are suitable for all children. We have suggested teaching pupils how to learn, how to think and how to problem-solve. We have coupled this with encouraging all learners to understand the ways in which they learn most effectively. If this teaching and learning is embedded in a curriculum that is relevant to the pupils, responding to their learning needs in detail, then progress, at whatever speed and in whatever direction, should be possible.

So we are saying that there is little that is different about teaching pupils with learning difficulties from teaching any child. Different pupils require different amounts of support and different access to the curriculum, will have different outcomes from their learning, will perhaps experience different environments or activities from others but their basic learning needs are the same. There is no magic and special formula to teaching pupils with learning difficulties that can only be provided by an expert. Effective teachers will be continually observing, evaluating and theorising about all the children they teach, whatever their needs. Reflecting in this way is vitally important and should accompany teachers throughout their careers. We hope that the principles embedded in this book, and the suggested ideas and examples, will provide a starting point.

References

Allen, J. (1999) *Actively Seeking Inclusion: Pupils with Special Needs in Mainstream Classrooms*. London: Falmer Press.

Ashman, A. and Conway, R. (1993) *Using Cognitive Methods in the Classroom*. London: Routledge.

Atkinson, D., Jackson, M. and Walmsley J. (eds) (1997) *Forgotten Lives: Exploring the History of Learning Disability*. Kidderminster: BILD Publications.

Babbage, R., Byers, R. and Redding, H. (1999) *Approaches to Teaching and Learning: Including Pupils with Learning Difficulties*. London: David Fulton Publishers.

Barton, L. (1997) 'Inclusive education: romantic, subversive or realistic?', *International Journal of Inclusive Education* **1**(3), 231–42.

Bayliss, P. (1998) 'Educating Ben: thought, language and action for children with poor language abilities'. In Burden, R. and Williams, M. (eds), *Thinking Through the Curriculum*. London: Routledge.

Beveridge, S. (1996) *Spotlight on Special Educational Needs: Learning Difficulties*. Tamworth: NASEN.

Beveridge, S. (1999) *Special Educational Needs in Mainstream Schools* (2nd edn). London: Routledge.

Birtwhistle, J. (1998) 'Reading Recovery'. In Burden, R. and Williams, M. (eds), *Thinking Through the Curriculum*. London: Routledge.

Blagg, N., Ballinger, M. and Gardner, R. (1988) *Somerset Thinking Skills Course Handbook*. Oxford: Blackwell.

Blamires, M., Robertson, C. and Blamires, J. (1997) *Parent-Teacher Partnership: Practical Approaches to Meeting Special Educational Needs*. London: David Fulton Publishers.

Booth, T. (1996) 'Stories of exclusion: natural and unnatural selection'. In E. Blythe and J. Milner (eds), *Exclusions from School: Interprofessional Issues for Policy and Practice*. London: Routledge.

Bristow, J., Cowley, P. and Daines, B. (1999) *Memory and Learning: A Practical Guide for Teachers*. London: David Fulton Publishers.

Brown, E. (1996) *Religious Education for All*. London: David Fulton Publishers.

Burden, R. (1998) 'How can we best help children to become effective thinkers and learners? The case for and against thinking skills programmes'. In Burden, R. and Williams, M. (eds), *Thinking Through the Curriculum*. London: Routledge.

Byers, R. and Rose, R. (1996) *Planning the Curriculum for Pupils with Special Educational Needs*. London: David Fulton Publishers.

Carpenter, B., Ashdown, R. and Bovair, K. (eds) (1996) *Enabling Access: Effective Teaching and Learning for Pupils with Learning Difficulties*. London: David Fulton Publishers.

Cline, T. (1992) 'Assessment of special educational needs: meeting reasonable expectations'. In T. Cline (ed.) *The Assessment of Special Educational Needs: International Perspectives.* London: Routledge.

Collis, M. and Lacey, P. (1996) *Interactive Approaches to Teaching.* London: David Fulton.

Coupe, J., Barton, L., Barber, M., Collins, L., Levy, D. and Murphy, D. (1985) *Affective Communication Assessment.* Manchester: MEC. Available from Melland School, Holmcroft Road, Manchester M19 7NG.

Creese, A., Daniels, H. and Norwich, B. (1997) *Teacher Support Teams in Primary and Secondary Schools.* London: David Fulton Publishers.

Croll, P. and Hastings, N. (1996) 'Teachers matter'. In Croll, P. and Hastings, N. (eds), *Effective Primary Teaching: Research-based Classroom Strategies.* London: David Fulton Publishers.

Crowther, D., Dyson, A. and Millward, A. (1998) *Costs and Outcomes for Pupils with Moderate Learning Difficulties in Special and Mainstream Schools.* Sudbury: DfEE Publications.

Dean, J. (1992) *Organising Learning in the Primary School* (2nd edn). London: Routledge.

DfE (Department for Education) (1994) *Code of Practice on the Identification and Assessment of Special Educational Needs.* London: HMSO.

DfEE (Department for Education and Employment) (1997) *The SENCO Guide: Good Practice for SENCOs.* London: DfEE.

DfEE (1998) *Meeting Special Educational Needs: A Programme of Action.* Sudbury: DfEE Publications.

DES (Department of Education and Science) (1978) *Special Educational Needs: Report of the Enquiry into the Education of Handicapped Children and Young People* (The Warnock Report). London: HMSO.

DES (1981) *Education Act 1981.* London: HMSO.

Falconer-Hall, E. (1992) 'Assessment for differentiation', *British Journal of Special Education* **19**(1), 20–3.

Farrell, P. (1997) *Teaching Pupils with Learning Difficulties: Strategies and Solutions.* London: Cassell.

Feuerstein, R. (1980) *Instrumental Enrichment: An Intervention Program for Cognitive Modifiability.* Glenview, Ill.: Scott, Foresman & Co.

Fisher, R. (1995) *Teaching Children to Learn.* Cheltenham: Stanley Thornes.

Fitz-Gibbon, C. (1988) 'Peer tutoring as a teaching strategy', *Educational Management and Administration* **16**, 217–29.

Fortnum, H., Davis, A., Butler, A. and Stevens, J. (1996) *Health Service Implications of Changes in Aetiology and Referral Patterns of Hearing Impaired Children in Trent 1988–93.* Report to Trent Health, Nottingham & Sheffield: MRC Institute of Hearing Research and Trent Health.

Fox, G. (1998) *A Handbook for Learning Support Assistants: Teachers and Assistants Working Together.* London: David Fulton Publishers.

Galton, M. and Williamson, A. (1992) *Group Work in the Primary Classroom.* London: Routledge.

Gardner, H. (1983) *Frames of Mind: The Theory of Multiple Intelligences.* London: Heinemann.

Griffiths, M. (1994) *Transition to Adulthood: The Role of Education for Young People with*

Severe Learning Difficulties. London: David Fulton Publishers.

Grove, N. and Peacey, N. (1999) 'Teaching subjects to pupils with profound and multiple learning difficulties', *British Journal of Special Education* **26**(2), 83–6.

Hardwick, J. and Rushton, P. (1994) 'Pupil participation in their own records of achievement'. In Rose, R., Ferguson, A., Coles, C., Byers, R. and Banes, D. (eds), *Implementing the Whole Curriculum for Pupils with Learning Difficulties*. London: David Fulton Publishers.

Hart (1996) *Beyond Special Needs*. London: Paul Chapman.

Hastings, N. (1996) 'Classroom motivation'. In Croll, P. and Hastings, N. (eds), *Effective Primary Teaching: Research-based Classroom Strategies*. London: David Fulton Publishers.

Hogg, J. and Lambe, S. (1988) *Children and Adults with Profound Retardation and Multiple Handicaps Attending Schools or Social Education Centres: Final Report on the Needs of their Families, Foster Parents and Relatives*. London: Mencap.

Hohmann, M. and Weikhart, D. (1995) *Educating Young Children*. Yipsilanti: High/Scope Press.

Hornby, G. (1995) *Working with Parents of Children with Special Needs* London: Cassell

Keefe, J. (1989) *Profiling and Utilising Learning Style*. Reston, VA: National Association of Secondary School Principals.

Keefe, C. H. (1996) Label-Free Learning: Supporting Learners with Disabilities. Maine: Sternhouse.

Kerry, T. (1982) *Effective Questioning*. London: Macmillan Education.

Lacey, P. (1998) 'Multidisciplinary teamwork'. In Tilstone, C., Florian, L. and Rose, R. (eds), *Promoting Inclusive Practice*. London: Routledge.

Lacey, P. and Lomas, J. (1993) *Support Services and the Curriculum*. London: David Fulton.

Lewis, A. (1999) Integrated Learning Systems and pupils with low attainments in reading, *British Journal of Special Education* **26**(3), 153–7.

Lewis, J. and Wilson, D. (1998) *Pathways to Learning in Rett Syndrome*. London: David Fulton Publishers.

Lorenz, S. (1995) 'The placement of pupils with Down's Syndrome: a survey of one northern LEA'. *British Journal of Special Education* **22**(1), 16–19.

Lorenz, S. (1998a) *Children with Down's Syndrome: A Guide for Teachers and Learning Support Assistants in Mainstream Primary and Secondary Schools*. London: David Fulton Publishers.

Lorenz, S. (1998b) *Effective In-Class Support: The Management of Support Staff in Mainstream and Special School*. London: David Fulton Publishers.

Lyons, C., Pinnell, G. and Deford, D. (1993) *Partners in Learning: Teachers and Children in Reading Recovery*. New York: Teachers College Press.

Norwich, B. (1990) *Reappraising Special Needs Education*. London: Cassell.

Norwich, B. (1996) 'Special needs education or education for all: connective specialisation and educational impurity', *British Journal of Special Education* **23**(3), 100–4.

O'Hanlon, C and Turner, B. (1998) *An Investigation into the Factors Associated with the Failure of Educational Placements for Children with Down's Syndrome at both Primary and Secondary Level* (a report for the Down's Syndrome Association). London: DSA.

Pickles, P. A. C. (1998) *Managing the Curriculum for Children with Severe Motor Difficulties*. London: David Fulton Publishers.

QCA (Qualifications and Curriculum Authority) (1999) *The Review of the National Curriculum in England: The Secretary of State's Proposals*. Sudbury: QCA Publications.

Reid, G. (1998) 'Promoting inclusion through learning styles'. In Tilstone, C., Florian, L. and Rose, R. (eds), *Promoting Inclusive Practice*. London: Routledge.

Riding, R. and Rayner, S. (1998) *Cognitive Styles and Learning Strategies*. London: David Fulton Publishers.

Rose, R. (1991) 'A jigsaw approach to group work', *British Journal of Special Education* **18**(2), 54–8.

Rose, R., McNamara, S. and O'Neill, J. (1996) 'Promoting the greater involvement of pupils with special needs in the management of their own assessment and learning processes', *British Journal of Special Education* **23**(4), 166–71.

Salisbury, C., Galucci, C., Palombaro, M. and Peck, C. (1995) Strategies that promote social relations among elementary students with and without severe disabilities in inclusive schools, *Exceptional Children* **62**, 125–37.

SCAA (1996) *Planning the Curriculum for Pupils with Profound and Multiple Learning Difficulties*. London: SCAA Publications.

Souza, A. (with Ramcharan, P.) (1997) 'Everything you ever wanted to know about Down's Syndrome, but never bothered to ask'. In P. Ramcharan, G. Roberts, G. Grant and J. Borland (eds), *Empowerment in Everyday Life*. London: Jessica Kingsley Publishers.

Staff at Rectory Paddock School (1982) *In Search of a Curriculum*. Sidcup: Robin Wren Publications.

Stevens. A. (1997) 'Recording the history of an institution: The Royal Eastern Counties Institution at Colchester'. In D. Atkinson, M. Jackson and J. Walmsley (eds) (1997) *Forgotten Lives: Exploring the History of Learning Disability*. Kidderminster: BILD Publications.

Sylva, K. (1994) 'School influences on children's development', *Journal of Child Psychology and Psychiatry* **31**(1), 135–70.

Tod, J., Castle, F. and Blamires, M. (1998) *Individual Education Plans: Implementing Effective Practice*. London: David Fulton Publishers.

UNESCO (1994) *The Salamanca Statement and Framework for Action on Special Needs Education*. Paris: UNESCO.

Ware, J. (1996) *Creating a Responsive Environment*. London: David Fulton Publishers.

Watson, J. (1996) *Reflection Through Interaction: The Classroom Experience of Pupils with Learning Difficulties*. London: Falmer Press.

Watson, J. (1999) 'Working in groups: social and cognitive effects in a special class', *British Journal of Special Education* **26**(2), 87–95.

Wedell, K. (1995a) 'Making inclusive education ordinary', *British Journal of Special Education* **22**(3), 100–4.

Wedell, K. (1995b) *Putting the Code of Practice Into Practice: Meeting Special Educational Needs in the School and Classroom*. London: Institute of Education, University of London.

Williams, M. and Burden, R. (1998) 'Pulling it all together: the challenge for the educator', in Burden, R. and Williams, M. (eds) *Thinking Through the Curriculum*. London: Routledge.

Wood, D. (1998) *How Children Think and Learn* (2nd edn). Oxford: Blackwell.

Wright, H. and Sugden, D. (1999) *Physical Education for All: Developing the Physical Education in the Curriculum for Pupils with Special Educational Needs*. London: David Fulton Publishers.

Further reading

Bearne, E. (ed.) (1996) *Differentiation and Diversity in the Primary School*. London: Routledge.

Beveridge, S. (1999) *Special Educational Needs in Mainstream Schools* (2nd edn). London: Routledge.

Blamires, M. (ed.) (1999) *Enabling Technology for Inclusion*. London: Paul Chapman.

Byers, R. and Rose, R. (1996) *Planning the Curriculum for Pupils with Special Educational Needs*. London: David Fulton Publishers.

Carpenter, B., Ashdown, R. and Bovair, K (eds) (1996) *Enabling Access: Effective Teaching and Learning for Pupils with Learning Difficulties*. London: David Fulton Publishers.

Fox, G. (1998) *A Handbook for Learning Support Assistants: Teachers and Assistants Working Together*. London: David Fulton Publishers

Hart, S. (ed.) (1996) *Differentiation and the Secondary Curriculum: Debates and Dilemmas*. London: Routledge.

Tilstone, C., Florian, L. and Rose, R. (eds) (1998) *Promoting Inclusive Practice*. London: Routledge.

Wood, D. (1998) *How Children Think and Learn* (2nd edn). Oxford: Blackwell.

Appendix – Useful addresses

Organisations

NASEN
NASEN House
4/5 Amber Business Village
Amber Close
Amington
Tamworth B77 4RP
Tel: 01827 311 500

BILD
Wolverhampton Road
Kidderminster DY10 3PP
Tel: 01562 850 251

MENCAP
123 Golden Lane
London, EC17 0RJ
Tel: 020 7454 0454

Computer centres

ACE Centre (Aiding Communication in Education)
92 Windmill Road
Headington
Oxford OX3 7DR
Tel: 01865 763508
Fax: 01865 759810
Email: ace-cent@dircon.co.uk
Website: www.ace-centre.org.uk

BECTA
Milburn Hill Road
Science Park
Coventry CV4 7JJ
Tel: 024 76416994
Fax: 024 76411418
Email: Darren_Maynes@becta.org.uk
Website: http://www.becta.org.uk

Granada Learning (SEMERC)
Granada Television
Quay Street
Manchester M60 9EA
Tel: 0161 8272927
Fax: 0161 8272966
Email: granada.learning@granadamedia.com
Website: www.semerc.com

Computer software
Widgit Software Ltd
102 Radford Road
Leamington Spa
CV31 1LF
Tel: 01926 885303
Fax: 01926 885293
Email: literacy@widgit.com
Website: www.widgit.com

Index